BASIC BOOK OF CARNATIONS & PINKS

IN THE SAME SERIES

Chrysanthemum Growing
Dahlia Growing
Flower Gardening
Rock Gardens and Pools
Rose Growing
Vegetable Growing
Pruning
The Herbaceous Border
Decorative Shrubs
Weekend Gardening
Cloche and Frame Gardening

OTHER TITLES IN PREPARATION

Natural Gardening: no digging – composting and organic
Garden Pests and Diseases
Greenhouse Growing
Fruit growing

BASIC BOOK OF
CARNATIONS
& PINKS

W. E. SHEWELL-COOPER
MBE, NDH, FLS, FRSL, MRST, Dip.Hort.(Wye), DLitt

BARRIE & JENKINS
COMMUNICA-EUROPA

© W. E. Shewell-Cooper 1977

First published in 1977 by
Barrie & Jenkins Ltd,
24 Highbury Crescent London N5 1RX

ISBN 0 214 20395 6

Printed litho in Great Britain
by W & J Mackay Limited, Chatham

Phototypeset in Great Britain
by Filmtype Services Limited, Scarborough

Contents

Dedication
To
my friend the late
Montague C. Allwood, VMH, FLS
and
W. Rickaby of Allwood Bros, Hassocks,
for his help and advice

Acknowledgement
The author would like to thank Allwood Bros. (Hassocks) Ltd
for supplying all the black-and-white and colour photographs.

List of illustrations

Black-and-white photographs and line drawings

Preface

Although many people think carnations are summer flowers, it is possible to have them all the year round. They are colourful, fragrant and not difficult to grow. It has been my pleasure to visit a number of countries and advise carnation growers, both professional and amateur.

The British Carnation Society is the largest carnation society in the world. Readers who love carnations and pinks should join it – its address will be found in the Appendix.

No one could have been a kinder friend than the late Mr Montague Allwood of the well-known carnation growers, Allwood Bros Ltd, Hassocks. Fortunately his good work is still being carried on there and I am most grateful to all those at Allwoods, especially Mr W. Rickaby, who have given me help and guidance.

I would like to thank all those who have assisted in the planning, writing and production of this book, and particularly Mr Michael Hodson of Barrie and Jenkins – who takes such an interest in the whole Basic Book series. My thanks are due also to my secretary, Mrs Beryl Lovelock, for typing the manuscript.

W. E. SHEWELL-COOPER

Arkley Manor,
Arkley,
South Herts.

1 History of the carnation

My Gardener's Dictionary, published in 1763, says 'there are twelve sorts of dianthus, such as the botanists allow to be distinct species; and all the varieties of fine flowers which are now cultivated in the gardens of the curious are supposed to be only accidental variations which have been produced by culture.' On the other hand the *Rural Cyclopedia*, published in 1853, says of the dianthus, 'about 100 species of it, besides the innumerable varieties and the several hybrids of the carnation and the garden pink, exist within Great Britain; and all are beautiful, most are deliciously fragrant and many more inexpressively exquisite.'

The botanical name of the carnation is *dianthus caryophyllus*, and the dianthus is the original species from which perpetual-flowering, border, cottage, malmaison, picotee, Marguerite and Chabaud carnations have come. In addition there are innumerable hybrids. *Caryophyllus* means 'nut-leaved', referring to the clove scent of the flowers rather than to the shape of the leaves themselves. It was the great Swedish botanist, Linnaeus, who gave the name of dianthus (from Greek *dios* – divine, and *anthos* – flower) to this particular genus.

The dianthus was certainly known to the Romans, and was probably brought to Britain by the conquering Normans – possibly in the form of seeds in stone imported from Caen for building castles at Deal, Dover and Rochester. In 1286 we find the Earl of Lincoln growing pinks in Holborn. Chaucer mentions clove pinks in his *Canterbury Tales*, and so does Shakespeare in *A Winter's Tale*. At this time the flower was known by several variants of the old country name gillyflower. By the sixteenth century they were found in most gardens. John Gerard, in his *Herbal* of 1579, states that the new yellow-flowered kinds came from Poland. We are indebted to a wealthy London merchant and carnation-lover, Nicholas Leat, who imported new kinds at that time from German gardeners who had collected, by 1599, some sixty different varieties.

Queen Elizabeth I said that her two favourite flowers were the carnation and the rose and this undoubtedly encouraged the

11

hybridists at that time to improve the range of colours. It is said that Charles I grew over sixty varieties of dianthus in his Whitehall Palace Gardens. By the time that Charles II came to the throne in 1660, there were 160 different varieties of dianthus, and in 1676 more than 360 varieties had been listed. This was a great improvement on John Parkinson's list of 1629 which only included nineteen varieties of carnations and thirty of 'gillyflowers'.

In the 1830s a famous French nurseryman called Lacene produced, by means of a cross, the Remontant carnation, which has played a great part in fathering the true perpetual-flowering carnations as we know them today. Another Frenchman by the name of Alegatière was the first person to increase his stock of carnations by cuttings instead of layers. It was from his nursery in Lyons that many plants were imported into Britain; they were then known as tree carnations. Some were sent to the USA in 1850, and were given the name of 'American carnations'.

In 1895 a Massachusetts grower called Peter Fisher produced a very beautiful deep rose pink variety, and there was great excitement in the horticultural world when an American millionaire, Thomas W. Lawson, bought the complete stock and named it Mrs T. W. Lawson. This was the first really good quality perpetual-flowering carnation. When it was eventually imported to Britain, it caused quite a sensation because it had stronger stalks, larger blooms and finer lasting petals than any variety previously known.

Perpetual border carnations were not introduced until 1913. Malmaison carnations start their history in France as one of the Remontants; they were popular because they produced very large highly-perfumed double flowers, but they lost their appeal when it was discovered that they didn't flower in the winter and were rather delicate from the point of view of culture. There is now a better type of Malmaison that has arisen as a sport from one of the perpetual Malmaisons.

Pinks have been known since the 1590s. In the mid-seventeenth century some sixty varieties were available. They were given some wonderful names like Puck, Cob Pink and Bandoleer, but unfortunately they have not survived. From the eighteenth century we probably have that old-fashioned variety, Mrs Sinkins, often wrongly called Mrs Simkins, and Ruth Fischer – both are double whites. In the nineteenth century their popularity decreased but about fifty years ago Montague Allwood succeeded in crossing the perpetual-flowering carnation with the variety of pink known as Old Friend, to produce the allwoodiis. The progeny had the best traits of both parents – they were perpetual-blooming, richly fragrant and sturdy but dwarf in growth. The allwoodii has in its turn been used as a parent to produce perpetual-flowering alpine pinks, and has even been crossed with a sweet william to give us the Sweet Wivelsfield.

2 Soil and Composts

There are five main types of soil found in British gardens, and these are usually described as (a) clay, (b) sandy, (c) loamy, (d) limey (alkaline) and (e) peaty. A clay soil is smooth and silky to the touch, but even when well drained it is apt to be wet. If it is worked when sodden, it may set like cement, when it will be very difficult to cultivate. It is best, therefore, to dig a clay soil shallowly in the autumn and leave it rough so that winter frosts will pulverize the exposed lumps of soil and make them easy to fork and rake in the spring. Clay soil should be given regular dressings of lime because this helps to open it up and make it more workable.

A sandy soil is light and dry, but it is easy to cultivate. It is much warmer than a clay soil, but it is poorer in plant foods, especially potash. A sandy soil can, however, be very acid and regular dressings of lime are therefore needed. Sandy land is invariably short of organic matter and so heavy quantities of well-rotted compost or sedge peat have to be used each season. In this way sandy soil can be encouraged to hold moisture better.

The loamy soil is the ideal blend of clay and sand. It is the kind of soil which all gardeners would like to have. A loam has all the advantages of clay and sandy soils and none of their disadvantages. On the other hand, a loam may well need dressings of lime as well as regular applications of fully rotted compost.

A limey (alkaline) soil is usually rather shallow, and lacking in humus and plant foods. It is often sticky and unpleasant to work when wet, but it has one advantage in that it is not acid and so needn't be limed. This kind of soil, however, does need heavy dressings of organic matter incorporated into the top few inches each season.

The peaty soils found in many parts of Britain and particularly in Somerset, Cheshire and Lancashire are often waterlogged. They are very acid, and lime has to be given each season; they are, however, full of organic matter and it is not usually necessary to add compost. Plant food can, however, be given

14

organically in the form of a fish fertilizer.

If I were asked to describe the soil which pinks and carnations like best, I would undoubtedly choose a well-drained good medium loam to which the right amount of lime had been given. Fortunately, it is now easy to test soil for its lime content, using the soil indicating fluid available from chemists and garden shops. This is a green liquid which when applied to soil, will quickly turn yellow, orange or red if acidity is present. The aim of the carnation grower is to see that the soil has a pH value (this is a measure of soil acidity or alkalinity) between 7 and 8. (See Glossary.)

Some readers may feel that their soil doesn't fit into any of these categories, and it is true that when a garden has been cultivated for, say, thirty years or more, especially in towns, it tends to contain blackish or greyish soil. This kind of land can be helped by digging in quite rough organic matter such as lengths of straw cut into pieces about 6 in. long. These can be laid into the trenches upright during digging, and they provide the right type of aeration. Other old garden soils are so 'puddingy' that they are improved by forking in coarse silver river sand (not sea sand because it is too salty). Dig this land shallowly in November and leave the clods really rough for the frost and winds to act on them. If too much lime or wood ashes have been used, then the land could be too alkaline even for carnations or pinks. Don't use lime for a number of years, but apply a seaweed manure at 5 oz to the square yard and bonemeal at 3 oz to the square yard.

If you have been growing pinks and carnations for a number of years in the same bed, rest the land for a season or two and use some other crop. Plants excrete from their roots toxins which can be slowly poisonous to themselves. Thus the gardener calls land 'cauliflower-sick', 'strawberry-sick' or, in this case, 'carnation-sick'. A thorough change of cultivation will undoubtedly improve the tone of the soil. Aim, therefore, not to grow members of the dianthus family on the same piece of land more than six years running; after that, crop the bed with other flowering plants and particularly, if possible, members of the legume family, such as sweet peas and annual lupins.

Under glass in beds

In the greenhouse most carnation growers prefer to grow their plants in beds at soil level. This allows the plants to grow as naturally as possible and to produce flowers with a good length of stem. Dig the soil over shallowly, to a depth of, say, 6 in. The soil should be enriched with a large quantity of powdery, properly composted vegetable refuse. Put this all over the ground as a layer 3 in. thick, and rake or fork it in lightly. This is far better, in fact, than burying the dung or compost in the trench as you dig.

Ground limestone must now be added at 1 lb to the square yard, as a top dressing; it need only be raked in lightly. This will not be necessary if the soil is very limey – make a simple test with the soil indicator as mentioned above.

When preparing the border, kill all soil pests like wireworms, which can be very destructive to newly planted carnations. In a newly prepared bed, wireworms will have no other plant roots to feed on and so they will really go for the carnations. Impale a few cut carrot pieces on a cane, and bury them 1 in. deep. Pull them up after three or four days to see if the wireworms have burrowed in. If they have, pull them out and drop them into a tin of paraffin. Then bury the carrots again and examine them once more 3 days later.

In addition to the compost an organic carnation fertilizer with an organic base, such as a specially-prepared fish manure, should be used at 8 or 9 oz to the square yard; this is a very heavy dressing. It can be forked into the ground at the same time as the compost, for it should be incorporated before insecticidal dust is used and certainly before the surface dressing of carbonate of lime. After all these various dressings have been given, the soil should be firmly trodden down and allowed to settle for four or five days. Place on this firmed base a 3in. layer of No-Soil compost.

There is one more point to be borne in mind during the first digging, and this concerns the moisture content of the soil. If the land is dry – and it often is in a greenhouse – you will need to fill each trench with water as you dig. A garden hose can be used to flood the land trench by trench; in fact this is the only way of ensuring that the sub-soil is properly moistened. It is important to water at digging time and not to wait until the compost is applied.

If the greenhouse soil consists of heavy clay, buy special growing compost. Alternatively, make your own from the following ingredients: 8 parts of good old turfy loam (preferably sterilized), 2½ parts of medium sedge peat, and 1½ parts of coarse silver sand; add to this mixture 12 lb of hoof and horn meal or meat and bonemeal, and 2½ lb of ground limestone per cubic yard.

If the soil is a light sand, the growing compost should consist of 9 parts old turfy loam (preferably sterilized), 1 part medium sedge peat, and ½ a part of coarse silver sand; add 12 lb of meat and bonemeal and 2½ lb of ground limestone to each cubic yard. Again, you can buy this ready made up.

Allow the compost to settle for three or four days after placing it over the original dug earth; then firm and rake it to get a good tilth. Some gardeners build brick or concrete walls 6 in. high around the beds in the greenhouse in order to retain this growing compost, which is by then, of course, above the general level of the paths on either side of the bed.

Incidentally, there are 21 bushels of soil to a cubic yard, and a rectangular box 22 in. long, 10 in. wide and 10 in. deep holds one bushel of the compost exactly. Remember that this kind of compost is put on the ground to form 3-in. deep beds for the carnations. In fact, therefore, the quantities of base required are ½ lb per square yard and of limestone ¼ lb per square yard.

Using special compost ensures that the two main root diseases, fusarium wilt and verticillium wilt, do not give any trouble. (See Chapter 11.) Even in old greenhouses, you can prevent the roots from getting into contaminated soil by using the growing compost in beds with side walls and false bottoms and increasing its depth to 6 in.

Some experts grow carnations satisfactorily in pure sand or gravel, and provide all the necessary plant foods by means of sub-irrigation. They claim that they have no trouble with diseases and soil pests; they don't have to do any watering or weeding, and yet just as many flowers are produced. The snag, of course, is that the equipment is too expensive for most gardeners.

Under glass in pots

Many gardeners don't want to grow their carnations in beds – their greenhouse may be needed for other plants as well. They are perfectly happy to grow a number of different varieties in pots on the staging of the greenhouse, along with other foliage and flowering plants. The compost used should consist of loam, peat and sand of the right kinds and proportions for texture; add fertilizers for nutrition. The loam used should be sterilized – the process is described later in the chapter, for gardeners who want to do it themselves. The main John Innes Potting Compost consists of 7 parts by bulk good sterilized loam, 3 parts by bulk medium grade sedge peat, and 2 parts by bulk coarse silver sand; add to each bushel of this soil mixture ¼ lb of John Innes base and ¾ oz of ground chalk. The John Innes base consists of 2 parts by weight of hoof and horn – ⅛-in. grist; 2 parts by weight of superphosphate of lime; and 1 part by weight of sulphate of potash. This should give an analysis of 5·1 per cent nitrogen, 7·2 per cent soluble phosphoric acid and 9·7 per cent potash.

Lately the author has great success with using the Alex Soilless Compost, which can be obtained ready for use. It is often difficult today to obtain the correct sterilized loam to make up to JIPC, and the Alex Composts solve the problem.

This mixture is officially known as the John Innes Potting Compost No. 1 (JIPC 1). John Innes Potting Compost No. 2 (JIPC 2) is the same compost but with twice as much John Innes base and ground limestone per bushel prepared. John Innes Potting Compost No. 3 (JIPC 3) – once again, it is just a question of adding three times as much of the JI base and lime to the compost as in JIPC 1.

Rooted cuttings of carnations do best in JIPC 2, and there is no need to start them off in JIPC 1 as there is for other kinds of plants. With carnations, I like to reduce the number of pottings-on to an absolute minimum, and so I use JIPC 2 as the main compost for growing carnations in pots. In fact, I invariably plant the rooted cuttings straight into permanent pots. Some gardeners prefer to pot up the rooted cuttings into 6-in. pots, using JIPC 2 and taking care not to plant too deeply. When the plants are well established, 6 or 7 weeks later, they pot them on into the 8-in. pots in which the carnations are going to grow and flower, using JIPC 3. They keep the plants fairly dry until the roots become settled in their new pots.

In the open in beds

A carnation bed in the open needs to be dug and prepared in the same way as beds under glass. But you won't need to put a growing compost on top of the soil. Dig the ground over, burying powdery, brown-black, well-rotted compost a few inches deep, at one good bucketful to the square yard. Rake into the top 2 or 3 in. a medium-grade sedge peat in the same quantities, plus a fish fertilizer which should be applied at 5–6 oz to the square yard. Tread the bed well, and when the surface is level give carbonate of lime at 5–6 oz to the square yard or whatever quantity may be necessary as a result of soil tests with the **BDH** soil indicator.

In sandy soils and light loams you can dig and plant in the autumn. With heavy soils, however, it is better to delay planting until spring, say, early April. There are in fact varieties of border carnations which prefer being planted in April whatever the soil.

Soil Sterilization

If you want to make up your own John Innes compost, the loam should be sterilized. This means destroying weed seeds, insect pests, disease spores and harmful soil bacteria. The method used is to bring the soil up to a temperature of 205–210 degrees F, and then to cool it down quickly. The useful nitrifying bacteria which are so important are not affected because they are able to produce hard-walled spores which can resist heat.

You can buy an electric sterilizer, or use the following cheaper method. Put 2 gallons of water into a large kitchen vessel. Hang 2 in. above this water a metal bucket perforated all over with ⅛-in. holes, 2 in. apart. The bucket can be supported on any kind of framework which lets the steam through. Fill the bucket with the loam that is to be sterilized, and boil the water in the vessel. Keep the top covered and try to get the water to the boil in about 10 minutes. The loam should then be at a temperature of 180–200 degrees F half an hour later. After this, continuous steaming for 5–10 minutes and the soil will be sterilized.

3 Propagating carnations and pinks

All carnations and pinks can be propagated by seed but, with
the exception of the annual types dealt with in Chapter 00,
seedling raising is not worthwhile to the amateur gardener. If a
grower wants to raise new varieties, he only sows the seed which
has been produced after careful cross-pollination. The seed is
usually sown in pans or boxes filled with JISC or Alex No-Soil
compost, and put into a greenhouse in April at a temperature of
about 63 degrees F. Once the plants have been raised, it is
possible to increase them by means of layers or cuttings.

In general, the various types of carnations are propagated as
follows:

Chabauds	By seed sowing
Border carnations	By layering
Picotees	By layering
Malmaisons	By cuttings or layering
Perpetual-flowering carnations	By cuttings
Pinks	By pipings

Seed Sowing

All types of carnations, pinks and dianthus can be raised by seed
sowing. It is not possible, however, to produce named varieties
in this way. Buy or make up the following John Innes seed
compost: take 2 parts by bulk sterilized loam, 1 part by bulk
sedge peat, and 1 part by bulk coarse silver sand; when this is
thoroughly mixed, stir in 1½ oz of superphosphate of lime
containing 18 per cent phosphoric acid and ¾ oz of ground
chalk per bushel. (Remember that a bushel is the quantity of
soil or compost that fills a box 22 in. long, 10 in. wide and 10 in.
deep.)

One bushel of John Innes seed compost or Alex No-Soil
compost will fill nine nursery seed trays 2 in. deep, 14 in. long
and 8½ in. wide. If you prefer 3-in. deep boxes, you can fill six
trays. Sow seeds in February, to plant out in April.

Fill the boxes to within ¼ in. of the top with the compost.
Then sow the seed of the Marguerite or Chabaud carnations

very thinly over the top. Sift a little more compost through a
⅛-in. sieve, so as just to cover the seeds. This light covering
should then be pressed down slightly with a wooden presser.
Now immerse the boxes very carefully in a bath of tepid water
until you see the moisture coming to the top. Don't dip them in
too quickly, or the compost will be loosened and may even be
pushed out of position.

Put the boxes on the staging of the greenhouse at 45–50
degrees F, covering each one with a sheet of glass and a piece of
newspaper. The glass keeps the seedlings warm and doesn't let
moisture escape, while the newspaper excludes the light until
the seedlings appear. Every day the glass should be removed;
any moisture that has collected on the inside should be wiped
away before the glass is replaced. When all the seedlings are
through, take away the glass and the paper. At this stage give
the boxes a light watering through the fine rose of a can.

Too much heat is not desirable, and the aim should be to
grow the young seedlings on as coolly as possible. Once the
seedlings are ½ in. high the boxes can be placed on the shelving
of the greenhouse near the lights for about a fortnight; then they
should be put out into a sunny frame where they can be gradually hardened off. Generally speaking, however, carnations are
not tender and in most parts of the country you can plant them
out in the open about the end of March or early April.

If the plants are put into a well-prepared bed in a sunny spot
in April, they should start to flower from July onwards. I have
sometimes sown batches of seed in boxes of Alex Soilless compost early in June, and germinated them in a sunny frame. The
plants were then over-wintered under dutch lights or cloches,
with the result that really first-class plants were available for
setting out in the open in March. These flowered a fortnight or
so earlier than those raised from sowings under glass in February.

The seed of border carnations can be sown early in June. The
aim is to put the plants out where they are to flower in late
summer. If they are planted in a sheltered border, they will live
through a normal winter because they are quite hardy. They
will then flower quite early the following year and can be left
undisturbed in the bed, to go on flowering for three or four years
if necessary.

If you are interested in sowing seeds of perpetual-flowering
carnations as a challenge, make sure you buy them from a
reputable, preferably specialist, stockist. Sow the seeds in the

Seed is very expensive to produce. Once harvested, it is hand winnowed through a machine to cleanse the seeds from the husks, after first being loosened by a spatula, as shown in the photograph

greenhouse in February, using Alex Soilless or John Innes compost as described above for Marguerites or Chabauds. You should get most of the plants in bloom by September. By October the inferior seedlings can be weeded out, and you can keep the types you like.

The seedlings should be through in 10 days' time and you can then remove the glass and paper. With these types of carnations, you must prick the seedlings out 2 in. apart into other boxes filled with JIPC or Alex Soilless compost; if you prefer you can pot them straight into 3-in. pots containing a similar compost. Don't try to stop the plants by pinching out the growing points. Let them flower straight away; then you can discard the singles and the plants with the poor-coloured flowers. If you were to stop the plants, you would not be able to choose the ones you liked until much later.

If you don't want to keep your perpetual-flowering carnations in the greenhouse the whole time, plant them out in a bed and watch them carefully. By late September it should be possible to select the best varieties and to pot the plants up into 6-in. pots filled with JIPC 2 or Alex Soilless compost.

It is not worth trying to raise perpetual-flowering carnations from seed unless you are really keen, because it is quite a gamble. It takes a long time, and from two or three sowings you may easily discover that there are only one or two plants of any merit at all. If you haven't got a heated greenhouse, you can sow the seeds of Marguerite and cottage carnations in late spring or early summer in boxes containing JISC, or in Alex compost in frames. Allwoodii seedlings are often raised in a similar manner, while the seeds of the various species of dianthus, when sown in boxes, usually take a long time to germinate. For this reason many gardeners place them in a shady spot in the open, covered with a flat board. When germination eventually takes place, they are moved to a frame and the final pricking up is done when the plants are a ½ in. or so high.

You can sow seeds of pinks in a sunny open position out of doors in early summer. Rake fine sedge peat into the surface of the soil at a bucketful to the square yard, and if the land is heavy apply coarse silver sand at a similar rate. Steamed bone flour should be worked in at the same time, at 4 oz to the square yard and, if the soil is at all acid, carbonate of lime should be applied at a similar rate. Seedlings raised out of doors in this way must be given some protection against bad weather. For instance, they don't like too much sun and they don't enjoy being beaten down by a heavy rainfall. Expert growers, therefore, protect the seedlings once they are through by stretching sheets of butter muslin over the beds, held about 1 ft above the ground, or using cloches.

About the third week of September the seedlings raised in this way can be planted out where they are intended to grow and flower. Pinks are usually in bloom within seven months of seed sowing, but border carnations may not be in flower for eight or nine months. I have known cottage carnations in flower in six months from seed sowings made in the spring.

Layering

This is usually carried out on border and cottage carnations, though it can be used for pinks too. It depends to a certain extent on the weather, but it is usually all right to start layering at the end of July and to go on with this method of propagation, if necessary, right through to the middle of August.

The cambium cells in a stem (the cells that can heal by forming a callous) are more concentrated around the stem joints or nodes. This callous will easily form new roots, so layering is done by cutting through the centre of a stem just below a node or joint. Thus the bisected node starts to form roots while it is still attached to the parent plant and receiving the necessary elaborated sap.

The reasons for getting the layers made and the plants struck in late July or early August is that you get nice sturdy specimens which can be easily potted up and over-wintered into a cold frame, and that the peak of the first flowering should be past, which means that much of the elaborated sap is concentrated on the vegetative shoots which are the ones chosen for layering. If you start to layer earlier than this, the plants are too leggy and cannot easily be accommodated in the frame space while there may be few of the right type of vegetative shoots to choose from. On the other hand, if you layer too late, the weather may be wrong and rooting will not take place strongly enough.

Loosen the soil around the fringe of a perfectly healthy plant (it is very important to propagate only from perfect specimens – striking layers from plants that are riddled with red spiders or attacked by some fungus disease only leads to disappointment). Having removed some of the soil in a circle around the plants, put in its place a little mound of JIPC 1 or Alex compost. Alternatively, use some sterilized loam mixed with equal proportions of sedge peat and silver sand – the sand will keep the mixture open.

Whichever compost you use, make it quite firm around the chosen plant; then select the non-flowering shoots that are to be layered and strip off the lower leaves. Stripping should always be done with an upward rather than a downward pull, because if you pull downwards you may cause the skin to tear. Make an upwards cut with the sharp blade of a budding knife right into the centre of this stem, starting just below a node and ending just above a node. A tongue should be formed, and if you trim it a fair amount at the base you can expose a little more inside flesh, with the restul that there will be more callousing and rooting.

Now bend the stem down, keeping the cut open all the time. Use a hairpin or bent wire to peg the layer above the cut, pushing the cut surface well in below the compost. The hairpin ensures that, when the rooted plant is removed later, the roots themselves will not be injured. This idea is that the layered shoots should be buried only 1 in. deep in a 2-in. depth of compost, which must be made firm. Some gardeners, therefore, just peg down into the original ring of compost that has been put in position; then, when they have completed the number of

A well-rooted layer

layers required, they put a further 1-in. layer of compost on top.
You can, of course, take a dozen or so layers from each plant but
each one must be stocky and sturdy – never try to propagate
from straggly growth. It is best to make the cut where there are
five good pairs of leaves above; then when the struck layer is
separated from its parents, it should have six good pairs of
leaves which can manufacture enough elaborated sap to keep it
going.

If the weather is dry (and it often is in August), see that the
compost around the plants is kept watered regularly. Apply the
water through the fine rose of a can or from an overhead
sprinkler or square area rainer. If the compost is kept on the
moist side and the weather is warm enough, rooting will take
place comparatively quickly and the layer plants can be separated from their parents after five weeks. In good years I have
known some varieties to be ready in three or four weeks.

Sever the young plants from their parents two or three days
before actually moving them. In this way they will get over the
shock of being separated while they are still in the same spot,
and they start to obtain on their own all the plant foods they
need. Dig up the young plants with a trowel, disturbing the
roots as little as possible and leaving them in a good ball of soil.
They can then be planted out into the beds in which they are to

grow. The roots can then get well established before the winter sets in.

If your soil is very heavy, or you live in a particularly cold, wet district, it may be advisable or indeed necessary not to plant out in the autumn but to pot up the layered plants, in JIPC 2 or Alex Soilless compost, in 3-in. pots. The pots can then be over-wintered in a frame or cold greenhouse, and planted late in March or early in April the following year.

Always remember that carnations are really quite hardy and you can even harm them by attempting to coddle them. When they are growing in the greenhouse, they should always be given plenty of ventilation and should never grow in an atmosphere that has been allowed to become stuffy or humid. When the beginner tries to coddle carnations they invariably suffer from rust and mildew.

Cuttings

A cutting is a small shoot cut from an existing plant in order to produce a new plant. It is essential for a cutting to have a large enough reserve of food stored within it, which will enable it to stay alive while new roots are being produced. Perpetual-flowering carnations are invariably propagated by cuttings, which are taken any time from the middle of October to the end of February. Some commercial growers have had good results with cuttings taken in March. Cuttings of outdoor carnations, pinks, alpine pinks and allwoodiis are usually taken from late May or early June until early September. I get the best results from cuttings taken in late May and in late September – they never seem to root quite so well in the heat of the summer.

Whichever type of plant is being propagated by cuttings, it is vital to select shoots that are not flowering at the time. The best cuttings are those taken from the sturdy side shoots and not the leading growths. Once again, it is important only to choose completely healthy plants from which to propagate.

Make sure that the roots of the plants from which cuttings are taken are not suffering from drought. It is very difficult to get cuttings to root quickly if they are taken from plants which are dry. The plants may be removed from their parents with a slight downward pull. They usually come away with a small quantity of the parent's bark attached. If a long strip of bark comes away, the cutting will be too hard to root **properly**; if none comes away at all it is too soft.

It is never advisable to take cuttings from the tops of plants or right from their base. The best cuttings come from about half-way down and good propagators select those that are sturdy and have short internodes between the leaves. Experts often keep selected plants specially for the purpose of providing cuttings, and the may not allow these to flower. If cuttings are taken haphazardly from any plants, disease or weakness may be passed on. Strong-growing isolated stock plants, as they are called, produce strong, healthy cuttings.

Cuttings taken from perpetual-flowering carnations should be 3–5 in. long. Cuttings from dwarfer plants like alpine pinks need only be 1–2 in. long. Each cutting should have about four fully-developed leaves. Use a sharp-bladed knife or a razor blade and sever the cutting from the shoot on which it is growing

Taking a cutting

Cutting after it has been trimmed. It is now ready for potting in

with a straight cut just at or below a node. Trim off the short curly leaves for about ¾ in. up, and do the same with any tail of bark there may be on the heel of the cutting. The main idea is to remove the parts of the leaves that would touch the sand when the cutting is pushed in. There must never be any jagged edges to let in the disease. Push the cutting into pure silver and deep enough to make it stand upright. Some people prefer to use sharp silver sand, with one-fifth of its bulk in fine sedge peat. Others root their cuttings successfully in vermiculite which, when washed, may be used again and again. Sand, however, must be used fresh for each batch of successive cuttings.

The sand (or sand and peat, or vermiculite) should be put in deep pans or pots and firmed level to within ¼ in. of the rim or top. The rooting material should be at least 2 in. deep and there should be a 4-in. layer of broken crocks below, for drainage. When hundreds of cuttings are being taken, they can be struck 2 in. apart on the rooting material, which is spread evenly on a propagating bench. If you are just taking a few cuttings, you will find they strike easily if they are dibbled around the edge of a pot as shown in the drawing.

Cuttings strike best when there is bottom heat from hot water pipes or electric heaters which can give a temperature of 60–65 degrees F. The general air temperature of the house above, however, may be as low as 55 degrees F. Never leave the cuttings in the sand or vermiculite longer than is absolutely necessary; the moment the plants have rooted well they should be potted up into 3-in. pots, using JIPC 2 or Alex compost. The cuttings will root in about 28 days on average. One or two varieties may be ready to pot up in 23 days, and some kinds, in some years, are extremely obstinate and take about 35 days.

If you want to take a number of different kinds of cuttings, it is quite a good idea to make up a little frame and put it on the staging of the greenhouse. The frame can consist of a bottomless box, 9 in. deep, into which you place about 3 in. of broken crocks, and on top of that 2 in. of pure coarse river sand or vermiculite. Dibble the cuttings into this and put a sheet of glass over the top to cover the box completely. The glass can then be slid off slightly to let in a little air when the cuttings start to strike. Incidentally, this propagating box should be put in the part of the greenhouse that gets the maximum amount of sun in the winter. A box is used because it prevents draughts blowing on to the cuttings – an important factor – and of course a box like this is easy to shade from the sun. This doesn't mean to say that cuttings don't need sun – they do; but they do not want direct sunshine on them in the early weeks, because this makes them lose too much moisture by evaporation. Remember that they haven't any roots at that time with which to take up some more.

As I have already said, cuttings can easily be rooted around the edges of pots and pans. Make holes with a pencil, pointed stick or dibber, ¾ in. deep or so, and insert the cutting so that it rests firmly on the base of the hole. Firm the sand round it afterwards. Cuttings can be as close as 1½ in. apart all round the inside of the pot. After the cuttings are in position, water them lightly, which helps to settle the propagating material. The pot can then be planted right up to its rim in sedge peat, inside the propagating box; this prevents the sand from drying out too quickly. A sheet of glass, of course, goes over the top of the box, and for the first few days a sheet of newspaper adds the necessary shade. It may not be necessary to go on giving water until rooting has finally taken place – just keep the propagating material moist.

If you find it difficult to root carnation cuttings you can use synthetic hormones (in dust or liquid form). Use them according to the instructions on the packets or bottles.

If you want to take cuttings of pinks and allwoodiis, prepare them in the way already described and dibble them into a bed in a warm spot out of doors. The bed itself must be well drained and it helps if coarse silver sand and fine sedge peat are forked into the top inch or so at the rate of 2 bucketsful to the square yard. The bed should be trodden down well afterwards and watered thoroughly. Dibble the little cuttings in on a 2-in.-square basis and shade them by hanging up sacking until rooting actually takes place. Some gardeners cover these out-door cuttings with whitewashed cloches for the first few weeks.

All cuttings, whether of carnations or pinks, must be gradually hardened off when they come out of the propagating case. This will get them used to the ordinary atmosphere of the greenhouse.

Leaf cuttings

Select a cutting of seven or eight joints, and next to it make an incision down the stem between the pair of leaves in order to peel them away, taking care, however, that the axil or base still adheres to the leaves. This is important, for if the axil does not

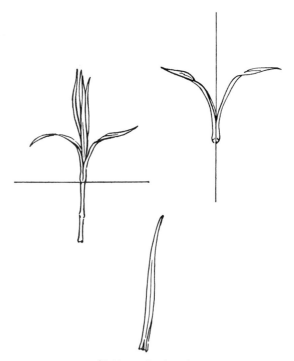

Taking a leaf cutting

adhere the cutting will be useless. Carefully trim the base of the pair of leaves with a sharp knife or razor blade – it should now be ready for inserting. Be sure to leave the embryo shoots – see drawing.

Leaf cuttings can be made at any time of the year, though it is better on the whole not to attempt to do this in the hottest period, say July and August. Leaf cuttings should be set in pure fresh sand.

Any soil mixture for carnations may easily get too acid, and therefore it is important to make up the John Innes compost each time it is needed – that is why I prefer an Alex compost – and not to store it for months on end. Old John Innes compost is liable to become acid and the great thing for the beginner is to learn to keep the pH right. When the pH is correct, then the plants do well.

Heel cuttings

Many people like to take their cuttings with a heel. The term 'heel' means a small portion of the older wood which is allowed to remain on the bottom of the younger wood used as a cutting. To make a heel cutting, get hold of a healthy, strong, non-flowering shoot about halfway down; pull it downwards and slightly sideways at the same time, and the shoot should sever with the necessary heel. With a sharp-bladed knife, cut back the base of the heel until it is only about ¼ in. long. Then remove three pairs of leaves at the base of the young wood just above the heel. Dibble it in firmly into an equal mixture of sand and damp sedge peat.

Heel cuttings should be taken immediately after flowering, some time in mid- or late summer. They usually root satisfactorily if they are treated as detailed on page 28.

Allwoodii cuttings

It is easy to propagate allwoodiis and many of the garden pinks, too, if sturdy, non-flowering shoots are selected from healthy plants and prepared as advised for ordinary cuttings. These may be dibbled in to the actual soil in which the allwoodiis are growing, close to the parent plants. The advantage is that the parents provide the cuttings with shade and the offspring then usually root without difficulty.

Alternatively, cuttings of allwoodiis and pinks may be dibbled in to a special cutting bed out of doors; this should contain good soil with fine sedge peat forked in at the rate of 2 bucketsful to the square yard. After forking, the bed should be trodden well and then given a thorough watering through the fine rose of a can. Dibble the cuttings in to this bed on the 2-in.-square basis, and put up a low hessian screen or a sheet of black polythene to provide shade until the cuttings root.

Readers with small gardens may prefer to fill a 6- or 7-in. pot with a compost consisting of silver sand and sedge peat in equal parts. Water this well, and press the compost down level until it is within ½ in. of the top of the pot. Then sink it into the ground in a shady sheltered spot. Dibble the cuttings in 1 in. apart around the edge of the pot, and invert another pot over the top of exactly the same size (or larger) until the cuttings are rooted.

Dividing the plants

As with all other herbaceous plants, it is usually possible to split up large specimens into two or three and then to transplant them into a new position. Sometimes, because the whole of the bushy growth seems to develop from one central stem only, division seems impossible. The only thing to do under such circumstances is to split up the plant into a number of 'branches' and to dibble the base of these branches into the soil wherever you want them to grow. This method is, however, not too reliable.

The best plan is to make up a compost mixture consisting of 1 part good soil, 1 part silver sand and 1 part sedge peat, and to place a couple of handfuls of this, after moistening, right in the centre of the plant to be divided. If this is done in June or early July and the mound kept moist by regular watering, the various stems of the carnation or pink will start to root in this medium. It is then a simple matter to dig the plant up in early October and to cut off the various stems, each one now rooted into the compost. These can then be planted out with every hope of success.

Sometimes (especially with the dwarfer-growing types of dianthus) the growths near the ground root of their own accord. Just divide them in the normal way.

Propagating pinks by pipings

The piping of a pink is a kind of cutting prepared by pulling the top growth of a stem out of its joint. It actually means pulling a stem apart at a node. Because the piping is pulled out of the node, it is automatically ready to be used as a cutting. I remove the two basal leaves of this piping, and then dibble it in around

A piping of a pink

the edge of the pot as described on page 29, or in a special cutting bed as described on page 30. Pipings are best taken in the summer.

4 Border carnations

No one should think that border carnations are difficult to grow. They are certainly hardy, and most modern varieties are robust; they will grow almost anywhere, provided they can have the air and sun that they love. Like all members of this family they hate an acid soil, and to give the plants a chance of getting going I would always advise planting in March when the ground is neither too sodden nor too dry. It helps if the carnations can be bought in pots or ex-pots; it is then a simple matter to remove the drainage material, tease out the roots to loosen them, and plant firmly.

Soil

It's all very well to lay down hard and fast rules as to what the soil should be – most of us have to put up with whatever soil we have in our gardens. Fortunately border carnations are not exacting and I have seen them flourishing in earth of varying textures. The lighter types are preferable because the plants then have the free drainage they love. If you have to cope with a very heavy clay soil, try and improve it by forking in sand, flue dust, anthracite ashes or the ashes of any other similar inert material. Coal ashes should not be used because they can contain poisons. Heavy soils can also be improved by forking in plenty of compost or sedge peat.

Sandy soils can be improved by working into them damped sedge peat, which shouldn't be too fine, at a bucketful to the square yard. Fine compost can be used instead (the idea, of course, is to incorporate some organic matter which will help retain the moisture). With heavy soils it is useful to raise the bed a little to ensure perfect drainage.

The well-known grower Montague Allwood always used to say that the perfect soil for border carnations was a fairly strong loam which was rich in humus and free from stickiness. If a bed was to grow border carnations year after year, it should be well dug so that compost could be added at the rate of about 2 bucketsful to the square yard, to a spade's depth. After digging

34

in the autumn, the land should be made rough, and in the spring before, it should be trodden firmly before planting.

Situation

Choose a nice open situation which receives direct sunlight and which is not overshadowed by buildings or trees. A south-west-facing position is ideal. If the soil is very heavy and drainage therefore likely to be bad, add fresh soil to the bed to raise it 6 in. or so above normal ground level. This soil in its turn must be trodden firmly.

'Clarinda', a hardy border carnation

Preparation and manuring

I have already talked about digging in the autumn and leaving the soil rough so that frost and cold winds can act upon it. This makes the ground easy to fork and to pulverize in the spring. At this time well-rotted compost or sedge peat can be added at, say, 2 bucketsful to the square yard. At the same time, make certain that the border is absolutely free from perennial weeds – it is impossible to grow any flowers if they have to compete with ground elder, creeping buttercup, couch grass or creeping this-tles. During digging, make certain also that the ground doesn't contain such soil pests as grubs of chafer beetles; and if you see any, fork an insect dust into the soil. You can also sprinkle this dust over a soil surface before you fork it over lightly in the early spring, say 14 days before planting. Having eliminated all perennial weeds and soil pests, an organic fertilizer can be added with an analysis of about 6 per cent nitrogen, 6 per cent phosphorus and 10 per cent potash. I use a fish-based manure with this analysis, and it has always been very successful. It is important not to force carnations, and so the organic fertilizer given should be one that releases its plant foods slowly. Some gardeners prefer to use their own mixtures and a good one consists of 1 part of meat meal, 2 parts of bonemeal and 4 parts of wood ashes. Use this mixture at the rate of 2 oz to the square yard.

In addition, it is useful to give regular dressings of fish fertilizer during the growing season – from the beginning of May until the beginning of September. It is never advisable to over-feed, and I like to give just ½ oz of fish manure to the square yard once every three weeks – each time the bed is hoed. It is important to sprinkle the fertilizer all over the ground and not just around the base of the plants themselves. Alternatively, you can use a liquid seaweed fertilizer. Don't forget, when preparing the bed, to give lime as a top dressing after the fish fertilizer has been forked in. It prevents acidity, supplies the calcium the plants need and helps to make a heavy soil more workable. The amount and type of lime to use depends on the acidity and type of the soil. In light soils, use carbonate of lime, i.e. ground chalk or ground limestone, but if the soil is heavy, and you can get hold of it, work in coarse mortar rubble, or a coarse type of ground chalk.

Planting

Some gardeners argue that planting should always be done in the autumn to give the roots a chance of developing before winter sets in. Others say that it is risky to plant in the autumn and it is far safer, especially for the beginner, to plant in March. The problem has been made more difficult by the fact that cross-breeding in the last few years with the less hardy yellow European varieties has produced a plant for which autumn planting is not advisable. However there are still numerous hardy types which can be planted in the early autumn with great success. A specialist nurseryman will tell you which varieties can be planted successfully in the autumn and which are better planted in March. Of course, it makes a difference whether the soil is light or heavy. A heavy clay soil is cold and damp and therefore it is often better to wait until it is warmer in the spring. Light sandy soil is warm even in the autumn because it is well drained; in this kind of soil, autumn planting is best. If plants are set out in a light sandy soil in mid-March, and there happens to be a drought in May, the carnations may suffer badly.

If you want to be quite safe, plant in March, as soon as the ground is fit to get on. If the land is sandy, be prepared to water regularly in a dry May or June and to apply sedge peat as a mulch all round the plants to the depth of at least ½ in. and for about 6 in. around them. In the north it may be as well to delay spring planting until April, but don't, whether in the north or south, delay planting until May, because you will only get poor flowers the first summer.

It is very important to plant firmly; the level of the ball of soil (which has just been knocked out of the pot) should be just about at the surface of the carnation bed. Don't plant deeply so that the base of the stem is covered, because you may encourage stem rot. Plant on the foot-square principle, though if you know that the variety is a very strong grower, give 15 in. either way. Even though you may have planted firmly in the autumn, remember that winter frosts can easily loosen plants, and it may be necessary to tread round the border carnations after a hard spell to make certain that they are firm once more.

First steps with new plants

Ask the nurseryman to let you have sturdy, short-jointed, firm-leaved specimens. The plants will probably arrive having been recently knocked out of 3-in. pots, and wrapped in newspaper or polythene. Unwrap them carefully and trim off any damaged or cracked leaves with a sharp knife. If there is a crock at the base of the ball of soil, remove it. If the plants have travelled some distance and the ball of earth on each is dry, moisten them thoroughly by standing the plants in a bucket containing a little water. An hour later it should be possible to plant them in the bed where they are to flower. Make a hole to fit the ball of soil perfectly, see that the roots are buried firmly but don't plant so deeply that the base of the stem is buried.

If you have raised your own plants from cuttings struck in the open ground, lift them by plunging a sharp trowel into the soil on either side of each plant so as to keep a good ball of soil on each one. Plunge the trowel in perpendicularly to cut a half circle on one side of the plant and then do the same on the other side. Lever slightly and the plant, with its roots, in their ball of soil, should come up whole. Plant as described above.

Lever slightly and the plant, with its roots, in their ball of soil, should come up whole. Plant as described above.

If you plant in the autumn, it may be advisable to push into the soil, near the carnation, lengths of cane about 9 in. long. Push the canes 3–4 in. deep into the soil and then tie the plants to their canes so that they cannot rock about in the winter time. The wind loosening plants in winter causes what is known as the 'wind rocking death' (water collects round the loosened roots and waterlogs them). This, incidentally, is another good reason for planting in March.

Propagation

It is usually agreed that the best time to root border carnation cuttings is during June and July. Layering is another first-class method that may be adopted, but take care that the layers never get dry during the rooting process. Get the necessary layering done in July and August; don't attempt it in September. Border carnations usually root in 3–5 weeks, provided the propagating soil which is placed around the plants is kept moist. Sever the layer from its parent plant at the end of that period, but do not attempt to pot it up until a week later.

Cultivation

Little needs to be done to border carnations other than to see that the plants are supported as they grow. You may find it convenient to give each plant a strong cane or galvanized rod with a movable galvanized ring, as shown in the drawing. This ring can be raised or lowered as you wish, to surround the various stems and blooms being produced. If you plant in autumn, put the supports in position by the middle of March; but if the carnations are not planted until the middle of March, the canes needn't be in position until the middle of April. Instead of buying sliding rings, you can support the carnations by pushing into the soil some twiggy pea sticks among which the stems can grow. Another alternative is to use a number of thin split canes – by pushing these into the ground at an angle around each plant, and joining the tops of the canes to one another with green twine, you can provide a circle to keep the blooms upright.

In the summer you must disbud them. Pinch off the laterals to let the main flower develop properly. At this time, too, you can thin out the growths if necessary, for sometimes the plants get too bushy. At the base of a disbudded growth, leave a side shoot

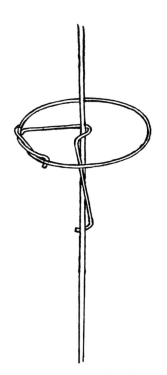

A galvanized ring-and-rod support

which may then be allowed to develop, so as to flower later. Don't attempt to pinch out the growing points of the shoots of border carnations; if you do, they will not flower the following year. Don't attempt to stop or tip the side growths, either.

In the autumn and early winter some of the long growths, which cannot possibly be in flower until the frosts arrive, may be pruned back. This will build up better plants for the following year. The idea, of course, is to grow the carnations on for about 4 years in the same bed before digging them up and replacing them. Some gardeners, it is true, look upon them as bedding plants, setting them out each autumn and discarding them the following autumn. In this way they raise new stock each year and find that they get much more compact plants as a result. It is true that, after the first two years, border carnations tend to become a little straggly.

Don't attempt to protect border carnations with mulchings of straw in the late autumn or winter. They do far better if they are exposed to the air and wind, for then the stems and the leaves will keep hardy and dry. After each hard frost, however, it does help to tread the ground around the plants, especially when they have been fairly new planted.

Don't forget that there should always be some non-flowering side growths making their appearance each late summer or autumn, which should provide the flowering stems for early blooming next year. Don't let these shoots be broken off by the wind – give them some support in late autumn.

Birds

In town gardens, especially, birds sometimes spoil the appearance of the foliage; stretch black cotton in and among the plants, between short lengths of cane. The damage is usually done during the winter, long before flowering.

Window boxes

If you are a town-dweller, you may like to know that border carnations have been grown successfully in window boxes for one season. Use normal JIPC 2 or Alex compost, but with Alex compost, generally speaking, a handful of lime should be added for each window box. Choose hardy, medium-growing varieties and plant them in the box firmly in late March or early April – staggered in a continuous V-shape so that they are about 1 ft apart.

If you don't stake them or tie them up at all, and forget all about disbudding, the plants will cascade down over the front of the box and look very beautiful from the street. If you prefer to keep their beauty for yourself, you will have to stake and support in the usual way.

Selfs and fancies

In some catalogues the fancies are not separated from the selfs (single-colour plants) but are merely described as varieties with, say, a yellow ground or a white ground. Other catalogues include, under the heading 'fancies', all the varieties with different ground to them other than the whites and yellows. The fancies are basically those which bear varicoloured flowers, other than the varieties which come under the definite heading of 'flakes' or 'bizarres'.

I shall keep to the usual catalogue arrangement, listing in Chapter 13 fancies (other than those with a white or yellow ground), yellow ground fancies, and white ground fancies.

Picotees

Picotees are just as hardy as border carnations, and some people would say hardier. They are certainly a distinct type, recognized by their flowers which are always either white or yellow, with a narrow band of colour right around the edge of each petal. Gardeners who grow picotees in large numbers say it is better not to disbud them, as they look better in sprays of three or four blooms to a stem.

You can grow them in a mixed flower border or in serried lines 1 ft apart to provide cut flowers. When grown in drifts in the border, they can be planted as close as 9 in. apart – nine or ten plants of one variety to a drift.

Their cultivation, planting, manuring and propagation is exactly the same as for border carnations. They should never be stopped or pinched back but they should be allowed to grow naturally.

Flakes and bizarres

A flake border carnation has a combination of two distinct colours. A bizarre border carnation, on the other hand, always has more than two colours. The bizarres and flakes are grown and treated in exactly the same way as normal border carnations. They can, if you like, be disbudded, and they will then produce beautiful large blooms.

5 Chabaud carnations

The term Chabaud carnations has unfortunately been used loosely for inferior quality strains of this plant – it is most important to get hold of seed of the original strain which resulted from the hybridization of the old perennial carnation and the annual wild or wood carnation by the French botanist Chabaud in 1870. Chabaud carnations with their large double flowers borne on strong stems are grown largely by cut flower growers in Britain and France. Many people call them by their original name, Marguerite carnations. They are easily grown from seed and you can have plenty of excellent flowers for cutting within 6 months of sowing. Some people say that the flowers do not last as long in water as the perpetual-flowering types, but against this it must be said that the blooms are very freely produced over a long period, and their culture is comparatively easy.

Seed sowing

To get these annual carnations to flower early enough in Britain, it is advisable to sow the seed late in January or early in February in JICS or Alex Soilless compost, in a greenhouse at a temperature of 45–55 degrees F. Use standard seed trays measuring 14 in. × 8½ in. × 2 in. (these are internal measurements). Nine of these shallow seed trays can be filled with 1 bushel of compost.

Put the compost in the boxes evenly and press down the corners as well as the centre. When the soil is level and within ¼ in. of the tops of the boxes, water it well and sow the seed thinly over the top. Press the seed in gently with a wooden presser and then sift a little more compost over the top, just to cover the seeds. Press this in lightly, too. Water the boxes lightly through the fine rose of a can and then stand them on the staging of the greenhouse, covering each one separately with a piece of glass, and putting over this a sheet of newspaper. Every morning remove the glass, wipe it and then put it back straight away. When the seedlings come through, remove glass and paper.

Just one word of warning with regard to the seeds themselves

– they are triangular in shape and slightly concave, and if they are not handled carefully they may crack or break. Make sure you buy the seeds only from a reliable firm, and order them just as you need them for sowing. It is better not to have them hanging about in a seed cupboard.

Pricking out

Watch the seedlings carefully, for they will need to be pricked out into new boxes when they are large enough to handle – this is when they start to make their second pair of true leaves. This may take place in 10–12 days' time, but in some years when the weather is dull it takes over three weeks. The boxes should be quite clean, and to make certain that they are disease-free (if they have been used before) dip them in a pan of boiling water for a minute or so. Though the outside measurements of the new boxes can be the same as the old ones, it is better for them to be 3 in. deep this time rather than 2 in. to give more root room.

Chabaud carnation seedlings that have been pricked out

The compost used may be the same as that used before, but I prefer to make up JIPC 1 or to use Alex Soilless compost. Firm the compost well in the boxes, until it is within ¼ in. of the top. Always firm the corners and the sides first and then the centre. Follow this by making the surface level with a firming board. In to this firmed, level compost prick out the little carnation plants so that the base of the leaves rests on the soil, and the roots are spread out to their full length. Each plant should be firm. Aim to have 54 seedlings to a standard seed box – do this by planting them exactly 1½ in. square. This enables you to get the maximum number of plants in the minimum space. Once they are in their boxes, syringe them with clean water, and cover them over with a piece of newspaper to shade them – this reduces the transpiration of the leaves to a minimum. When the leaves are firm and turgid, after four days or so, the newspaper can be removed and the plants can be grown on, on the staging of the greenhouse, at a temperature of about 55 degrees F.

After this period try and harden the plants off gradually by putting the boxes into frames. Keep the frames closed for two or three days, and then ventilate them on all suitable days. Remember to close the frames down if the weather is snowy, frosty or foggy. Early in April in the south, and usually later in April in the north, the young plants can be removed from their boxes with a good ball of soil to their roots, and planted where they are to flower. One of the best ways of ensuring that each seedling has enough soil is to draw a sharp knife down lengthways in between the rows and then crossways in between the plants. Each plant then has its own little block of soil. If you do this four days before planting out, and water well afterwards, each carnation should come out easily with its cube of soil attached.

Planting out

Choose a warm, sunny border and dig the ground over to a shallow depth. Incorporate at the base of the trench well-composted vegetable refuse or well-rotted dung at one 2-gal. bucketful to the square yard. If the soil appears very dry give the compost, when in position, a thorough soaking with water.

Now allow the ground to settle as long as possible and, a few days before planting out the carnation seedlings, fork over the bed lightly – no deeper than 2 in. – and add at the same time fish manure at the rate of 4 oz to the square yard. It invariably pays to apply sedge peat at half a bucketful to the square yard also. Don't forget the lime which is usually needed. Give this as a top dressing in the form of carbonate of lime at 5–6 oz to the square yard. Plant the seedlings out 1 ft square.

Disbudding

You seldom need to support Chabaud carnations. With correct soil preparation and proper feeding they should grow sturdily and start to flower from the beginning of July, going on until the first serious frost. These annual carnations can be disbudded – just remove the side flower buds as they appear on the stem so as to leave the end bloom to develop on its own, to a larger size. As with all carnations, make sure you pull the buds off at a tangent to the main stem so as not to damage the guard leaf.

Alternative methods

Chabaud carnations can also be grown in a cool greenhouse as pot plants. The seed is sown, as already described, in January.

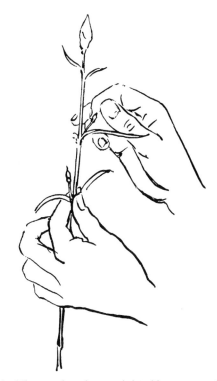

Disbudding so that the remaining blooms grow larger

When the seedlings are 1 in. high they are usually potted up into 3-in. pots containing John Innes or Alex Soilless compost. After another 8 weeks they are then potted up into 6-in. pots using JIPC 2. At this stage, be fairly generous with the lime. The plants will have to be supported with canes, and will flower successfully from about the middle of June until Christmas.

Another method is to plant the carnations out of doors and to let them flower there until early in October. Then select the best plants and pot them up into 6-in. pots using John Innes or Alex Soilless compost, providing plenty of crocks for drainage. Stake the plants, tie them round with green twine, and stand them on the staging of a cool greenhouse.

If you want Chabauds to flower very early, sow the seed during the middle of August in boxes filled with John Innes or Alex No-Soil compost. Sow the seed very shallowly, water it, and put the boxes into frames where the plants will grow slowly. Prick out the seedlings into other boxes when they are 1 in. high and grow them on in the frames until the following spring. At that time, of course, the plants are larger and those who use this system claim that the plants flower earlier in consequence.

Yet another method is to sow the seeds in a specially-prepared seed bed out of doors in a sunny, sheltered spot. The seed bed should be enriched with fine sedge peat at 1 lb to the square yard, plus fish manure at 2 oz to the square yard, and carbonate of lime at a similar rate applied as a top dressing. If you sow the seeds about the third week of August, then the seedlings should be covered with Access frames or continuous cloches early in October, for protection.

The following April, select from the seedling rows, which are usually made 6 in. apart, the sturdiest plants for planting out 1 ft apart.

Outdoor sowings

If you live in the south or south-west you can try sowing the seeds where the plants are to flower, and avoid pricking out and transplanting. You cannot do this unless the soil is very well drained, so if you have heavy clay you will probably have to have a raised bed. Choose a sunny position, work in manure and compost, and, when raking the surface level and making the top tilth, add fine bonemeal at 3 oz to the square yard.

The drills should be only ¼ in. deep and to do this the tilth must really be fine. After sowing, it is a good plan to cover the seeds with John Innes or Alex No-Soil compost rather than raking them in. The rows should be 1 ft apart, and when the seedlings are through the ground they should be thinned out to 9 in. apart in the rows. The seedlings can be transplanted to form other rows if necessary. In the very favoured spots in the south-west, sowing can be done in March, but in less-favoured situations, even in the south, April sowing is early enough. Raising the plants in this way, however, does make flowering very late.

Kinds and varieties

It is best to try and buy the seeds of the original strain. The varieties I recommend are listed in Chapter 13. If you do not want to buy the seed of individual varieties, buy a packet of mixed seeds, such as giant double Chabaud, which contains all kinds of coloured varieties.

COMPACT DWARF CHABAUDS

These dwarf Chabauds do not grow taller than 15 in. but produce fully sized, strongly scented double blooms. They are, therefore, excellent for window boxes, for edgings to borders or even for growing in pots for house decoration.

Unfortunately there are no definite varieties and it is necessary to buy a packet of mixed colours. Mauser's of Zurich, Switzerland have an excellent strain with large, scented blooms.

ENFANT DE NICE

This is a development of the giant Chabaud carnation and is said to surpass it in richness of colour and perfume. The plants are just as hardy and free flowering. The flowers have broad non-serrated petals, exceptionally sturdy stems and attractive grey-green foliage.

There are no definite varieties. Packets of seeds are available in specific colours, i.e. bright red, dark red, dawn pink, pink, mauve, salmon pink, white, yellow and striped. Packets of mixed Enfant de Nice seed can also be bought.

FLEUR DE CAMELLIA

This is said to be a strain of the giant carnation; its flowers strongly resemble the camelia. The character of the growth and the foliage itself is similar to normal Chabauds and the plants are very free flowering indeed. I know of no definite varieties.

MARGARITA

Margaritas are easily grown from seed, and flowers can usually be had within 5 months of sowing. The plants grow 15 in. high and for this reason are often used for bedding. There are no special varieties, but there is a strain known as iron stem mixed, whose flowers are considerably larger than the normal Margaritas. It contains a range of exceptionally bright colours and the flowers are produced on strong stems. Buy the seed of mixed extra quality Margarita.

TRAILING AND PENDULOUS CARNATIONS

These very beautiful carnations are ideal for hanging brackets, balconies and patios. They are a Swiss carnation, and seeds can be obtained from Mauser's of Zurich, although it is not possible to import cuttings into Britain.

The seed is sown in the same way as for Chabaud carnations, and the seedlings are treated similarly. Plants reared from seed have only 60–80 per cent double flowers, and it is only in the second year that they adopt a trailing habit. Ask for varieties like Ris d'Or, a yellow; Bernina; Schneeball, a white; Diable, a red; and Sortient.

6 Malmaison carnations

Malmaison carnations have a particularly glorious perfume. Some nurserymen today are working on the old Edwardian type of Malmaisons and have developed a wonderful strain with the same kind of fascinating perfume as the original Souvenir de la Malmaison. The leaves, on the whole, are broader, thicker and more rounded than the perpetual-flowering types, while the stems are shorter, stiffer and sturdier.

The old fashioned Malmaison is, of course, quite distinct from what are now called perpetual Malmaison carnations. The general cultivation of the latter is similar to the normal perpetual-flowering varieties, the only difference being, perhaps, that they require a little more heat – say 52 degrees F at night – especially during cold wet periods. Malmaisons need more skill in culture than any other kind. Those, however, who like a much stiffer type of plant, with broader leaves and massive blooms, should certainly concentrate on Malmaisons. The flowers are large and definitely double, and the centres are always well filled. A very large number of the varieties are pink. All varieties have a rich perfume though, because the calyxes are short and somewhat weak, they are apt to burst. The unopened buds of perpetual-flowering carnations are always long and pointed, while the buds of the Malmaisons are round and chubby.

The plants flower principally in the spring and summer and they are usually happy to rest in a deep frame in the winter or in a cool greenhouse. It is useful to be able to turn on a little heat to ensure a buoyant atmosphere and dryish air. It is also necessary to ventilate adequately and only to water the plants when absolutely necessary. In the frames the pot should be plunged 3 or 4 in. deep into coarse silver sand or fine ashes. In the greenhouse the pots will be on the staging, spaced out so that the air can circulate freely.

Propagation
This usually starts in June and is best done by layering. The plants are put out into the open air about the beginning of that

month. At the end of a fortnight or so the stems will be tougher, and will root more readily. Furthermore, because of this they don't break as easily when they are bent down into the layering position. Knock the plants out of their pots carefully and plant them in a frame so that the roots are completely buried but the stems are out of the ground. Plant firmly, so that there is plenty of room all round for the layers to be pegged down.

Now make up a compost mixture consisting of equal parts of sandy soil, fine sedge peat and coarse river sand. Put this round the plants, 3 in. away from the main stem and for a width of 2 in. to a depth of at least 1 in. Peg down into this compost the strong young side growths, as described in Chapter 3. It should be possible to treat six strong growths like this all the way round each plant.

Make a cut just above a node or joint, upwards to the next node. Keep the slit you have made open and peg it down with a bent wire or hairpin at least 4 in. long. It shouldn't be difficult to get these layers evenly spaced around each plant and to see that each one is fully covered with a 1-in. depth of soil. Make certain that the compost is damp by watering it thoroughly if necessary; go on watering every 2 or 3 days to keep it on the moist side. The layers should have fully rooted in a month's time and they can then be severed from their parent plants. Leave them for a further 10 days before they are dug up and moved.

I have propagated Malmaison carnations by making cuttings with a heel. These should be taken in December and rooted in pure coarse silver sand. The cuttings should have rooted properly by the third week of February, and potting up into JIPC 1 or Alex Soilless compost can be done late that month or early in March. On the whole, however, Malmaison carnations root far better from layers than from cuttings.

Potting up

Whatever the source of your plants, you must pot them up into 3-in. pots. If you have bought them, and they appear dry on unpacking, moisten the soil and roots well by putting them in a shallow container of water for 2–3 hours. The 3-in. pots used must be thoroughly washed and dried and should be carefully crocked. Be sure to put a hollow piece of broken pot over the drainage hole, concave face downwards and eight or nine smaller pieces of broken pot on top of this. Cover the crocks with a tablespoonful of coarse sedge peat before filling in with the compost.

Pot firmly and give each little plant a short piece of split cane to which the stems can be tied loosely to keep them upright. After potting, place the Malmaison carnations on a level, rough ash bed in a cold frame. If the weather is sunny, as it often is in July and early August, see that the plants are shaded for the first 4 or 5 days, from say 10.30 a.m. to 3 p.m. Cover the plants with sheets of newspaper or, if you have it, a length of butter muslin. The plants should be given a good watering when they are first stood on the earth, in order to saturate the soil, but after this give just enough water to keep the potting compost moist.

As winter approaches the plants should be kept on the dry side. It is quite a good plan to adopt the plunging method if you have used clay pots. Sand or sedge peat is used to a depth of 4 in., and the pots are then sunk into it; this has the effect of reducing pot evaporation to a minimum. As a result, it is seldom necessary to water more than once every 3 weeks. Plastic pots do not allow the evaporation of moisture through their sides, and so will not need to be plunged.

Potting on

Malmaison carnations must be watched carefully, for the roots can soon fill 3-in. pots. Generally speaking, potting on must take place at the end of 11 or 12 weeks. If, therefore, the first potting up is done early in August, because layering was done in the middle of June, then potting up into 6-in. pots would take place early in November. The plants therefore over-winter in their large pots rather than in their small ones. It is at this re-potting stage that plunging in sand, or peat can be done.

Use JIPC 2, not JIPC 1 but, apart from this, pot the plants up in exactly the same way as for 3-in. pots. Use a potting stick to ram the soil tightly around the outside of the original ball containing the roots and to have a layer of new compost over the sedge peat on which the base of the 3-in. ball of soil can rest. Finish off by tapping the pot lightly on the bench, to make the soil at the top level.

Stake the plants with short canes of the same height. After 10 days, give the pots a good soaking by standing them in a bath of water for an hour, to within 1 in. of their rims. From this time onwards, very little water will be needed during the winter period. Those who prefer can put the potted-up plants on the staging of a cool greenhouse instead of plunging them in sand or ashes in a frame as already suggested. When they are in a cold greenhouse, attention must be paid to the ventilation because they like to have fresh air on all suitable days, as mentioned elsewhere.

The plants in the frames will have ventilation also on warm, sunny days but the lights should be put on to keep off the rain and snow, and during exceptionally cold periods the frame may be closed down altogether. It is usually possible to raise the frame light on one side or the other during the winter, to allow the air to circulate freely.

Having grown the plants with plenty of air and maybe just a slight amount of heat to keep up the buoyancy of the atmosphere, it should be possible by the end of April to put the pots on the staging in the greenhouse, where the temperature can be kept at 55 degrees F at night. It will not be long before the flower spikes start to appear; the moment the buds start to open, the outside of the glass should be syringed with Verishade. The blooms of Malmaison carnations unfortunately bleach with strong sunlight, and therefore must be given shade throughout the summer.

Feeding

The moment the pot plants are placed on the staging of the greenhouse, regular feeding should begin. A liquid manure can be used, diluted in accordance with instructions given on the container. Each plant should be given ½-pt dose once a fortnight until all signs of flowering are over.

Second year

The moment flowering is over, select all the healthiest plants and cut the flower stems down to within 2 in. of their base. It is not worth trying to save poor, diseased plants for a second year. A fortnight after the cutting down, it will be possible to pot on the carnations firmly into 7-in. pots, this time using JIPC 3 or Alex compost. This is usually done during September. Syringe the plants regularly and water them carefully until they are well rooted in the new compost. Each new shoot, as it appears, must be carefully staked, so that by the middle of October it should be possible to put the staked plants into a deep frame as described for one-year-olds or, if preferred, to put them on the shelving of a cool greenhouse somewhere near the ventilator. The idea is to grow sturdy plants slowly during the winter.

When the time comes, i.e. at the end of the following April, the plants are again brought on to the staging of a heated greenhouse to flower. In the third year, they may be treated in a

Malmaison carnations

similar manner, i.e. they will be flowering in the summer on the staging of the greenhouse. Few people, however, keep Malmaison carnations in pots longer than three years; they much prefer to layer some of the plants each season, to keep up the vigour of the varieties grown.

Varieties
All varieties seem to have the general name of Souvenir de la Malmaison. But there are a number of definite kinds which I have seen growing in various parts of the country, and these are listed in Chapter 13.

7 Outdoor pinks and allwoodiis

There is perhaps no type of dianthus that has given greater pleasure to gardeners down the years than the ordinary garden pink. It is one of those truly English old-fashioned flowers that most of us know.

Fortunately pinks are easy to grow. In fact, they were once described to me as weeds. They are certainly not that, for they never like to remain in the same strip of ground for more than 2 or 3 years unless some new soil is introduced from another area. Pinks can be distinguished from carnations because they are dwarfer in habit, more compact in growth, and because their stems, on the whole, are thinner. All pinks have an eye in the centre of the bloom though it isn't easy to see on the doubles.

Pinks are on their own from the point of view of treatment in the herbaceous border. The typical perennial plant dies down in the autumn and springs to life in March and April each year. Shrubby plants keep their leaves in the autumn, or, like roses, shed them after one or two frosts. Pinks, however, are suffruticose – that is to say, they tend to be somewhat woody like a shrub but every little stem ends in evergreen leaves which go on growing except during the very frosty weather. Little branches may arise in the axils of the leaves and these flower in their turn.

It is best never to move pinks in the spring but to transplant them in the autumn, so that they get nicely established before the winter sets in. Always aim to get them moved and planted by the end of September, and you should have no trouble with them at all. It is better to buy small plants with really good roots than big plants with a poor root system.

Soil
Pinks will grow in any good soil. They hate land that is sodden and waterlogged and they equally dislike soil which is dry and droughty in the summer. Lime is not essential, and pinks can be seen growing quite happily in ground which is a little on the acid side. Pinks suffer far more from wet than from cold, so if you want to grow them in a heavy soil, make sure that the roots are never in sodden earth in the winter. You can easily achieve this

by making a slightly-raised bed so that the earth in which the pinks are growing is 6 in. or so higher than the soil around. Always use top soil, and don't attempt to use the sub-soil as a top dressing.

Medium grade sedge peat is very satisfactory for improving the soil structure if applied at the rate of 2 bucketsful to the square yard, and then lightly forked in. Fish manure should be added at the same time at 4 oz to the square yard. Then give carbonate of lime as a top dressing at the rate of 6–7 oz to the square yard if, having tested the soil with a soil indicator, it is found to be acid.

Pinks undoubtedly prefer to grow in a pH which is above the normal neutral level, that is to say, on the alkaline side. Because lime washes through so quickly it may be necessary to give more carbonate of lime the following year at 2–3 oz to the square yard. This again can be given as a top dressing. Aim to have the pH about 7·5.

Preparing the ground

There is no need to dig deeply for pinks, and forking over to a depth of 3 or 4 in. should do. It is at this stage that the peat and fish manure can be added. If the soil is very poor, and you want to add really well-rotted dung or compost, it may be advisable to dig up 5 or 6 in. so that the compost or manure can be added to the bottom of the spit. Digging is best done in the autumn, leaving the ground rough so that the frost and cold winds can act on it. This means, of course, that the actual planting has to be delayed until the spring – a delay which I do not favour. However, it is sometimes imperative to wait a year; the bed is prepared one autumn, it is cropped with some vegetable or annual flower the following spring, and then is planted up with pinks in the following mid-September. I prefer to fork shallowly, add the fish manure, and apply the powdery compost as a top dressing 1 in. deep.

Propagation

The normal method of propagation is by cuttings as described in Chapter 3, but inserted in sandy soil in a sheltered border in June or July, or in silver sand and sedge peat in a frame. These cuttings root readily. They are usually dibbled in about 2 in. square.

They may also be propagated by what are called pipings, which are really cuttings which are pulled out of a joint instead of actually being cut. It is a simple matter to get hold of the stem of a plant with one hand and then take the tip of that stem with the thumb and forefinger of the other hand, and firmly pull the top 3 in. of growth out of a joint.

Some gardeners like to take cuttings with a little heel; they use a razor blade to make a cut absolutely square well below a joint. Then they remove the bottom four leaves and push the 3-in. prepared cuttings into sandy soil, 2 in. apart, under a cloche or in a frame. Basal shoots should always be used for cuttings, and those which have not flowered. It is possible in July to strike cuttings in a sheltered north border especially if plenty of sand and sedge peat are forked in first. Under these circumstances, the cuttings are left where they are until September when the plants are put out in the beds where they are to grow.

Planting

Though I have just said that plants raised in the open can be put into their flowering positions in September, very often the work is left until March, and if necessary the plants need to be protected by Access frames or square glass cloches during the winter, particularly in the north. Whether planting is done in September or in March, the roots must not be buried deeply. The general rule is shallow but very firm planting. They will probably go in 1 ft apart and, as they resent being disturbed, the idea is to leave the pinks growing in the rows for many years. Every January give a light dressing of carbonate of lime at, say, 3 oz to the yard run, and every April fish manure may be applied at 4–5 oz to the yard run.

Cultivation

Set the pinks out in their beds 15–18 in. apart. If your aim is to allow them to grow for 4 years they will need to be 18 in. apart. Most of us, however, find that 3 years is enough, for plants get straggly even after the end of the second year. In the first season the bed can look under-planted; try planting baby gladioli corms in between – the effect is first class. This interplanting makes it more difficult to hoe, but it is well worthwhile. Very light hoeing is all that is necessary, just enough to keep down the weeds. The alternative is to mulch the bed with sedge peat ½ in. deep; this will smother annual weeds and provide the necessary mulch. Pinks hate dryness at the roots and so during droughty periods, where mulching is not done, they have to be watered every week. The advantage of mulching is that it prevents damage sometimes caused by hoeing too deeply. Far too many people allow the hoe blade to slip down to a 1-in. depth, and when this happens large numbers of pink roots are cut off. In the early autumn of the first season, it is quite a good idea to apply soot among the plants at two large handfuls per square yard.

In April each year go over the older plants to see if they have produced what are called winter buds. Remove these by cutting down the stems almost to their base – these flower buds always produce poor blooms and are a disappointment. Start the first hoeing, as a rule, about the middle of April, hoe again lightly 3 weeks later and on this occasion apply the fish fertilizer. If sedge peat is in position as a mulch, no hoeing will be necessary, but give fish manure as a top dressing about the beginning of May and let it get washed in by the rain. Some plants try and over-bloom, especially perpetual varieties; in this case, it is best to remove a third of the stems when the flower buds start to swell.

Supporting

The simplest way to support pinks, if it is absolutely necessary, is to use the twiggy pieces of pea sticks. Push the twiggy sticks in among the pinks so that they support the flowering stems without needing any ties. The leaves and the plants as a whole then screen the sticks and the supports are not too obvious. Don't use hundreds of little canes, which will make the pink bed look hideous.

Some pink devotees use the tops of michaelmas daisies, especially the taller varieties. The leaves are removed after the stems are cut and the stems are then stored in bundles in a dry shed. They are, of course, used in the same way as the tops of pea sticks. There are, of course, one or two varieties of pinks which do not need supporting at all; Gloriosa is one of them.

General remarks

Pinks make admirable cut flowers especially if the stems are not cut until the top bud (crown bud) has finished flowering. This can then be pinched off and the side buds will open – these are the ones that look best in vases. Do the picking in the evening, stand the flowers up to their necks in water in a cool room, cut the bottom of the stem slightly with a sharp knife to help water absorption and arrange the flowers the following morning. Pinks should last 12 or 13 days in water, especially if this water is changed every 2 days. Pinks add a fragrance to a room which is always noticeable and this is one of the reasons for their popularity.

Once the plants have flowered, it is as well to cut them back to keep them compact. Some gardeners go over the pinks once a week when they are blooming and cut back quite hard the individual stems of flowers that are dying. This helps the plants to go on blooming longer. Pinks are always apt to flop about and look untidy after they have been several months in the border, and it does no harm to keep them within bounds by cutting back straggling growths from time to time.

Varieties
Under this heading I am confining myself (as I have in the list in Chapter 15) to what I consider to be the true garden pinks. Some people may think I am old fashioned but I would rather recommend good old varieties which are beautiful and easy to

Single pinks

look after, than to suggest modern varieties which are not too good. These garden pinks can be grown on their own in a mass or they can be used as edging plants for the herbaceous border. All these pinks flower profusely in June and then rest until the following year.

In early Victorian times laced pinks were very popular indeed. They grow similarly to the normal garden pink, but all the petals are fringed with a contrasting colour. I never think they are quite as compact in growth as such varieties as Mrs Sinkins, but they are very beautiful and it is no wonder they are coming back into favour again. Raise them, propagate them, plant them, feed them and tend them in the same way as garden pinks.

Show pinks

In horticultural circles there has always tended to be a pull between the show bench and the garden. If a variety is very happy growing in a bed, it may not have long enough stems for show purposes, or the calyxes may split, or the blooms may not last well in water. The exhibitor demands far more, in fact, than the gardener. The Royal Horticultural Society is well aware of this, and they both (a) give awards for exhibits displayed in their halls or at the Chelsea Flower Show, and (b) carry out trials at their gardens at Wisley, so that experts can gauge how valuable the plants are in the open growing under normal conditions.

Latterly, there has been a tendency to divide pinks into two categories: the ordinary garden pinks already described, and show pinks, which are purposely grown to perfection to take their place on the show bench. It is the show pink, therefore, that is usually seen during the summer at horticultural shows. The show pink is, of course, a hybrid and it undoubtedly has a certain amount of allwoodii blood in it. Most of these pinks grow tall and, though they are by no means as free flowering as old friends like Mrs Sinkins, the blooms they produce are exquisite both in shape and colour. Many of the show pinks flower over quite long periods, and this enables the grower to exhibit at a number of shows throughout the summer.

The plants are by no means difficult to grow. They like to be planted in soil which has been double dug and to which properly composted vegetable refuse has been added at one bucketful to the square yard. In addition, a good fish manure must be raked into the top inch or two when the land has had time to settle. Finally, the ground should be made white with carbonate of lime. Plant in the spring, say late in March or early in April, in rows 1 ft apart, with 12 in. between the plants. If you want the pinks in a flower border, they can be arranged in drifts of five or six with the plants 9 in. apart.

As usual, plant firmly but shallowly. You should never allow moisture collect around the stems of the plants, so make sure that they are never set in a little saucer-shaped depression. Stake the plants when they need it, either by using a cane and garden raffia or by using a galvanized plant support as illustrated in the drawing on page 39.

Disbud the flowers as they appear, so as to produce the largest blooms possible. Feed once a fortnight from mid-July onwards with fish manure at 1 oz to the square yard only. It is seldom necessary to water the pinks, but if there is a drought during July or August, use a sprinkler. If you use it for about 20 minutes or half an hour, you get better results than if you just give little dribbles every now and then. Don't water unless it is absolutely necessary but, if you can, syringe the plants over in the evenings after hot days. This invariably does a great deal of good.

Allwoodiis

Allwoodiis are often known as perpetual-flowering pinks. They are really a hybrid of the old fashioned garden pink and the perpetual-flowering carnation. They are neat and graceful growers, not stiff or rigid, and they are very free flowering. They have an iron constitution and seem just as happy in the town as in the country. They have a long flowering season, and they produce blooms of brilliant colour which makes them popular as cut flowers. The more the plants are cut, the more they continue to bloom.

Allwoodiis will start to flower in the spring and continue through the whole summer and autumn. They make an ideal bedding plant for, apart from the flowers, they produce masses of glorious silver foliage which looks very attractive during the winter months. The plants can be grown in the same way as pinks, and can be propagated just as easily.

Propagation is usually done with cuttings, though it is possible to layer. Planting should be done in the spring, say late March, each plant being 1 ft from the next. Allwoodiis are all fragrant, but some are more richly scented than others and I have mentioned these in the list in Chapter 13.

'Arthur', a variety of Allwoodii which has a yellow ground

Imperial pinks

Mr C. H. Fielder of the Lindabruce nurseries in Lancing, Sussex, crossed the allwoodii with the Herbert pink, raised by the late Mr C. H. Herbert of Acres Green, Birmingham. The only worthwhile Herbert pink left is Bridesmaid, a flesh pink.

Imperial pinks are strong growers. They are good show varieties and have better branching habits of growth than the Herbert pinks. They are quite good for garden decoration, and by no means difficult to grow. They need stopping in the early stages to encourage branching. Propagation is by cuttings.

London pinks

Mr F. R. McQuown of the British National Carnation Society raised London pinks from crosses made with allwoodiis, garden pinks and Herbert pinks. There is some carnation parentage as well.

London pinks, on the whole, are laced, vigorous growers and free flowerers. Like imperial pinks, they branch better when they are stopped in the early stages; they are quite hardy and easy to grow. They are propagated from cuttings.

8 Rock garden pinks

I have purposely called this chapter 'Rock garden pinks' because after all this is a basic book and we want to keep it as simple as possible. Experts refer to the plant as *dianthus alpinus* or the alpine dianthus. Actually, of course, there are very large numbers of species of dianthus that are dwarf and grow happily in pockets in the rock garden or in between the cracks of crazy paving. There are also many hybrids which, if dwarf, are included in this chapter.

Many rock garden pinks have been collected from the mountains of Europe and particularly from the Austrian Alps. Most of them are easy to grow and just as easy to propagate – the dianthus family contains a very high percentage of types which can be grown under rock garden conditions. It is always difficult to lay down hard and fast rules, but generally speaking the tufted alpine kinds like to grow in sunny, open spots where the soil is on the dry side and may even, on the surface, be sunbaked. Dianthus, on the whole, dislike earth which retains moisture. They prefer well-drained, light soil with a layer of limestone chippings on top of the ground. If you plant these rock garden pinks in pockets, always be careful not to choose spots where moisture is likely to collect and cause trouble. It is better to select the rather upright crevices which are absolutely open to the sun, where the drainage is perfect and yet where the plants get some protection. Remember that they originally came from the higher parts of the mountains and so they love lots of sun, plenty of air and perfect drainage.

Never plant alpines in a rich soil because they will go soft and sappy. Don't let the plants become leggy and untidy; each year, after flowering, apply a top dressing of the following soil mixture ½ in. deep, and cut back some of the straggling branches if necessary – the compost used should consist of one-third sifted soil, one-third medium grade sedge peat and one-third coarse grit. Some people only include the sedge peat in the case of the few species that do not love lime – those from the highest parts of the Alps.

Early in October in the north, and about mid-October in the

south, a ¼-in. layer of limestone chippings, 2–3 in. wide, should
be placed around the collar of each plant. Once again, take care
in the case of the two or three species that dislike lime; use
sandstone chippings instead. The idea of using the chippings is
to prevent moisture collecting around the base of the plants,
which may happen in Britain but which cannot do so in the
Alps.

Buy the plants in the spring and ask for specimens with a big
root system and with small, strong, hardy, tufted tops. Make a
hole large enough to take the ball of soil and plant the pinks
firmly. Most of them will be in flower by late May or early June
and many will continue blooming until the end of September.
Many of the species are very fragrant and this adds to the charm
of the rock garden.

There is very little to do during the life of the plants other than
removing dead foliage from time to time, thinning out straggly
stems and stopping or pinching back growths which are too long
and leggy. Do this immediately after flowering – be fairly ruth-
less, use a sharp knife and cut back all the flowering growths
quite hard. You only need to leave a compact, tuft-like growth of
leaves to live through the winter.

Species and hybrids worth growing

DIANTHUS ALPINUS

This is one of the prettiest and dwarfest of the rock plants – its
large crimson flowers and light green glossy leaves look absolutely marvellous on the mountain slopes of Styria in Austria. In
Britain it produces flowers in late May or early June, and they
are huge for such a little plant. The stems are usually only
1½–2 in. high and they rise from low, mat-like specimens. Plant
collectors have seen forms with salmon-pink flowers and even
purple-pink flowers described as peacock-eyed. There are also
white forms which sometimes arise as the result of seed sowing.
In selecting seedlings, it is the ones with the lightest green leaves
that are likely to bear albino flowers.

It is a plant which loves an alkaline soil and, like all dianthus,
perfect drainage. It grows well in scree (see *Basic Book of Rock
Gardens and Pools*) and I have grown them successfully in open
compost in a stone trough. It is important to give the plants a
top dressing, as already described, at the end of September. Let
the compost trickle in thoroughly between the leaves and stems.
Water lightly afterwards through the fine rose of a can.

Unfortunately, *dianthus alpinus* is short-lived and therefore should be propagated by cuttings or seeds every 3 years. It is often very badly attacked by carnation fly maggots (see Chapter 11). Keep a sharp look out and treat the plants immediately. If you miss the initial attack the plants will wilt badly and get white markings on the leaves; it is better then to grub them up and burn them, to stop the trouble spreading.

DIANTHUS ALLWOODII ALPINUS

This is a race of sweet-scented, almost perpetually-flowering dwarf pinks. The plants have silvery moss-like foliage and a compact habit, usually growing not more than 6 in. high. They are usually fairly happy for 5 or 6 years in the same position. They are less disease- and pest-prone than the dianthus all-woodii. They are very fond of an open soil; if you have clay to cope with, burn some earth on a bonfire and incorporate this into the soil where the plants are to grow. In addition, limestone grit may be forked in at 2 handfuls to the square yard, and fine sedge peat at a bucketful to the square yard.

DIANTHUS ARENARIUS

This is included because it is one of the few alpine pinks that can be grown in a semi-shaded spot. It flowers over a long period; the blooms are usually very pale pink and slightly fringed. The stems are about 9 in. high.

DIANTHUS CAESIUS

This is usually called Cheddar pink and is a native of this country, though it is also found in the mountainous areas of Europe. It is very easy to grow and bears its rose pink twin flowers in profusion from June onwards; they are very fragrant. It is a lime lover and insists on sun and, if possible, a dry aspect. For this reason it is an excellent wall plant and is very good between the paving stones of a terrace, where it produces an attractive cushion with the flower stems about 4 in. high.

It is tidy; it seems to have no vices. It is easily propagated, it is very decorative and it is long lived, so what more can you ask in a plant? There is a variety known as Icombe which is even smaller and neater than the original *dianthus caesius*. In some catalogues, by the way, this variety is found under the name *dianthus glaucus*. I advise propagation by cuttings or division, and, for those who hope to get an unusual strain, by seed sowing.

'Hick's Triumph'

Perpetual-flowering carnations: ideal types for the amateur cool greenhouse

Perpetual-flowering carnations grown from seed

DIANTHUS CALLIZONUS

This is included because it is so attractive and because the flowering season usually extends into late autumn. It must have cool, gritty soil to grow in, and it likes to be top dressed twice a year in early June and late August with a mixture of sterilized soil and coarse silver sand in equal parts. The flowers are usually 1½ in. in diameter; they are lavender pink with a zone of dark dots in the centre.

When this species has been allowed to grow close to *dianthus alpinus*, a hybrid sometimes results which is called *dianthus calalpinus*. This is prostrate and bears long flowers on short stems, the foliage being a nice glossy green. It is easier to grow than *dianthus callizonus*.

DIANTHUS DELTOIDES

Usually called the maiden pink and probably one of the easiest alpine pinks to grow – if it has a fault, it is that it is too 'sprawly'. Give it a sunny situation in almost any soil and it will produce innumerable rose pink baby flowers from May to August. It has no scent. It must be given plenty of room in which to develop because it spreads so much. It will seed itself freely and some gardeners have told me it is so happy in their gardens as to be almost a weed! Grow it as a dry wall plant and it is delightful.

DIANTHUS FREYNII

Originally thought to be a form of *dianthus glacialis*, it is now regarded as a species. It is beautifully neat-growing, producing grey-green pincushions covered with pale pink flowers, though there is an albino variation. It is a long lived species if grown in poor soil containing lots of grit and ample ground chalk.

DIANTHUS GLACIALIS

This grows on the high alpine pastures in Switzerland and Transylvania (Romania). It produces glossy, broad, blunt leaves and bright carmine pink flowers on stems 6 in. high. It does not dislike lime, in spite of what some writers have said. There is a white form. Both this and the pink-flowered kind are at their best in July and August.

DIANTHUS HAEMATOCALYX

This is a very alpine pink which ought to be better known. It produces branching sprays and reddish purple flowers, the petals being yellow-backed and the calyx blood red. The plants are nice and cushiony and the flower stems about 8 in. high. It is at its best during July.

DIANTHUS KNAPPI

This is included because it is almost the only clear yellow dianthus; it comes to us from Hungary. The flowers, which are small, are borne in clusters on rather long ungainly stems. It seldom sets seeds, but when it does, they certainly come true. The foliage is grey-green.

DIANTHUS MUSALAE

This type takes its name from its place of origin, the Musal mountain in Bulgaria. It must grow in very poor soil or it won't live through the winter. It produces prostrate stems and grey-green leaves covered with glorious red flowers 1 in. in height, at their best in June and early July. Before planting *dianthus musalae* fork in limestone grit at a handful per square foot.

DIANTHUS MICROLEPIS

This only grows 1 in. high and produces myriads of minute pink or white blossoms. It is so small that it must be given a conspicuous position in the rock garden and taken care of. There is a variety called musaliae which bears red flowers.

DIANTHUS NEGLECTUS

This is an absolute gem. It is quite happy for years in one position, and it is easily raised from seed. It produces dense prosperous-looking tufts of short, fine leaves; the colour of the flowers may range from rosy pink to ruby red, but each one has a bluish black eye. These blooms are borne on stems of 3–4 in. in height. They usually appear first in June, but invariably give a brilliant show again in the autumn. Though it is said not to like lime, it certainly will grow in a calcareous soil providing it isn't too rich.

It is best to see the plants of this species in flower before actually buying them; there are some very poor strains, for the species seems to be variable. There are flowers, for instance, of salmon pink, and others of brilliant crimson. If you do manage to get hold of a good stock of this species, always propagate by division or by cuttings – cuttings preferably, because the *dianthus neglectus* doesn't like being disturbed. Never try to plant it in badly drained soil and don't add lime to the ground if it isn't there already. A good variety is Pike's Pink – a scented double, 4 in. high.

DIANTHUS MYRTEMERVIUS
This has pale green hummocks and pink flowers.

DIANTHUS NITIDUS
This Macedonian species produces purplish black buds on short stems, which open out into clear pink flowers 1 in. wide. There is a crimson line on every petal. It produces a tidy cushion of bright green leaves, and flowers well in June and early July.

DIANTHUS PETREUS
This type is sometimes wrongly called *dianthus kitaibelii*. Pale pink flowers are borne on stems 7–8 in. high. It produces a nice mat of dark green, almost prickly leaves and is at its best in June. After a few months, the stem may become rather floppy and ungainly. Some nurseries sell this species bearing single white flowers.

DIANTHUS RUPICOLA
Found in Sicily and southern Italy, it produces broad, flat, greyish-green leaves and grows compactly. The flowers are clear pink in colour and are produced in profusion on 2-in.-high stems during June and July. It loves sun and calm and hates wind and wet. It is therefore very happy in the Mediterranean and usually sad in Britain. Try it, however, in a pot in the greenhouse and you will love it.

DIANTHUS SIMULANS
This is said to be the dianthus which produces more blooms on one plant than any other species. The bluish-grey leaves form attractive-looking tuffets. The flowers, which are bright pink, look glorious on the mountainous slopes of the Greek-Bulgarian border from which it comes.

DIANTHUS SILVESTRIS
The flowers are clear rose pink, quite large but absolutely scentless. They appear, interestingly enough, on a mass of wiry arched stems and may be seen at their best from June until the early autumn. It's an easy species to grow and can be propagated by seeds or from cuttings. It prefers a lightish soil, plenty of sun but a minimum of lime; I therefore put sandstone chippings around this variety. It was previously known as *dianthus inodorus*.

DIANTHUS SUPERBUS

This bears masses of lavender or lilac flowers in various shades; the centre of each bloom is green. It is late-flowering and doesn't usually bloom until August. It is, however, an untidy grower with light green leaves and loose, straggly, almost tumbling stems. The variety Monticola comes from Japan and is in bloom in July and August. It only grows 6 in. high and its blossoms are fringed.

DIANTHUS VERSICOLOR

This may not be the original name of the plant, but it was sold as this and the name has stuck. It has lovely green leaves and the whole plant has a tufted appearance. It will produce masses of white flowers on stems 3 in. high; these start as pure white and then gradually turn to bright rose pink. As a result it is possible to see on one plant white and rose pink flowers as well as others at a midway stage between the two.

9 Dianthus Hybrids

One of the difficulties of talking about hybrids is that so many of their names have become household words that we have ceased to think of them as hybrids at all. Mrs Sinkins, for instance, is one of the best known hybrid pinks but most of us are content just to call it a pink and leave it at that.

In this chapter I describe a few hybrids which have not been dealt with in any previous chapter and which I think ought to be included.

The fact that a plant is a hybrid is usually shown by including the letter 'x' in front of the name – thus dianthus x A. J. Macself indicates that this is a hybrid whose original name is lost.

All the plants listed as dianthus hybrids in Chapter 13 should really be described as dianthus x or more simply as d.x.

Abbots Fordiana	Produces pale-pink semi-double blooms on 8 in. stems, from early July to mid-September.
Adoree	A clear rose with large flowers, often 2 in. in diameter. Stems 4 to 5 in.
Alba Fimbriata	Pure white, sweetly scented, deeply fringed hybrid. Stems 9 in. tall, flowers June to end of August vigorous grower.
Audrey Pritchard	Rose pink flowers, clove scented, stems 8–9 in. flowers June to end of August. Tufted habit, double.
Blairside Crimson	Produces single flowers often over 2 in. in diameter on sturdy 6 in. stems. Flowers deep pink with a crimson eye. Flowers late May to end July. Neat grower.
Cockensie	This comes to us from Scotland and is said to be the true 'Montrose Pink'. Lovely double-flowered variety, pink in colour. Season – July onwards. Stems 1 ft high.
Delmondham Fairy	Looks more like a carnation than a

	Pink, though it is definitely the latter. Shrimp pink flowers, scarlet eye.
Donezetti	Claret coloured flowers with deep claret eyes. Stems 9 in. Flowers from June to August.
Duchess of Fife	A clear rich pink, strong grower, late summer flowerer, single.
Elsenham Seedling	Good vigorous grower, large, pink single flowers with darker eye. Season late summer.
Floribundus	Rich rose pink, robust grower, stems 14 in., gorgeously scented, may flower too freely and so has to be restricted.
Fosteri	A rose crimson, leaves dark bronzy green, often over flowers, generally a poor doer and subject to maggot attack. Season July to August.
F. W. Millard	Dull crimson double flowers, stems 12 in. Strong grower with ash grey leaves. Seeds happily and the majority of the seedlings come true to type and colour.
Holmsted	Rose pink flowers 2 in. in diameter, stems 9 in. high, foliage of a beautiful green shade. Usually increased by layering or cuttings.
Little Old Lady	Very old white variety, neat grower, extremely fragrant, vigorous.
Princess Christian	Pure white, chocolate central zone, stems 1 ft. Season June to August.
Napoleon III	Cerise scarlet blooms, not a good grower. Difficult to propagate because all the shoots seem to produce a bloom. Season, June, July, August.
Raby Castle	Comes from Cumberland and is one of the oldest hybrids known. Red, semi-double flowers, with petals striped with black.
Windward Rose	Deep rose pink, ash-grey leaves, stems 6–7 in. tall, flowers throughout the summer, neat grower.

10 Sweet williams

The sweet william is included in this book because botanically it is the *dianthus baratus*. It is a very popular, hardy, ornamental evergreen herbaceous plant which is usually grown in British gardens as a biennial. The original sweet william was undoubtedly found in many parts of Europe; it is indigenous to Spain, the south of France, Italy, Greece and the southern USSR. Unlike the carnation, it has a bold, thick stem that stands firmly erect. It grows up to say 20 in., and bears a great profusion of brilliantly tinted small flowers in an inflorescence.

Soil
Like other members of the dianthus family, sweet williams like a well-drained loamy soil enriched with plenty of fine organic matter. Carbonate of lime should always be applied as a top dressing if there is any sign of acidity. Fork in old compost or sedge peat at a bucketful to the square yard; fish manure may be used at the same time at 3 oz to the square yard.

Situation
Sweet williams much prefer a sunny place. If you try to grow them in partial shade you will find that the plants tend to grow straggly and weak.

Preparation and manuring
Prepare the border with the manure mentioned above some time before planting. This gives the soil a chance of settling down, and by the time the plants are set out in their flowering position it won't be too loose and 'puffy'. Aim, therefore, to dig the ground over shallowly and leave it; then, in early spring, fork it in, adding sedge peat and fish manure, so that the border will be ready for planting early in April. If you have a light sandy soil you can plant out sweet williams in September, a week or so after the ground is prepared. It is only on heavy clay soils that it is better to postpone planting until the spring.

In either case, it is a good idea to give a second application of fish fertilizer at 2 oz to the square yard, in June when the flower stems are first seen. This will encourage better flower development, and those who like to take cuttings of any unusual specimens will discover that this fertilizer encourages the production of the right type of vigorous shoots for propagation purposes. These cuttings can be taken late in July, whereas layering usually takes place in August.

Raising the plants

The seed may be sown in early May, in a specially-prepared seedbed in a sunny place in the open. It pays to rake into the surface of the soil, sedge peat at half a bucketful to the square yard, bonemeal at 3 oz to the square yard and powdered carbonate of lime at a similar rate. If the soil is very heavy, coarse silver sand can be used at the same rate as the sedge peat. Having forked the ingredients in about 3 in. deep, the bed should be well trodden over or lightly rolled and the soil then raked level to produce a fine tilth. Drills should then be prepared 6 in. apart and ½ in. deep. This can be done very simply by laying the rake handle on the ground where the seed is to be sown and lightly treading it in to form a depression.

After sowing, rake the bed again lightly to cover the seeds; use the head of the rake up and down the rows to help firm the ground over the seeds themselves. If the weather is very dry, it pays to water the drills after they have been prepared, before the seeds are actually sown in them. Some gardeners sow seeds in JISC or Alex Soilless compost in boxes in the greenhouse in late April, or in cold frames at the end of the first week in May.

In all these cases, thin out the plants when they are large enough and set them out into nursery beds on a 6-in.-square basis. There they can grow quietly until they are transplanted.

Planting

By September nice sturdy plants should have grown in the nursery beds and they can be dug up with a good ball of soil to the roots. Transfer the plants to the place where they are to flower, the taller varieties at 12–18 in. apart and the dwarfs at 6–9 in. apart. As mentioned above, it may be advisable to delay planting until the spring where the soil is cold, wet and heavy.

Propagation

Normally the plants will be propagated by seed sowing and all the single varieties come true to type that way. The doubles can be propagated by cuttings or layers, as described for carnations in Chapter 3.

Cultivation

There is little to do with sweet williams other than to dutch hoe lightly in between the plants to keep down weeds. The plants do not need staking for they are strong enough to stand up on their own. If you are organically minded, put a 1-in.-deep mulch of sedge peat all over the ground after planting, and this will smother annual weeds, conserve the moisture in the ground and provide extra organic matter which the plants love.

Window boxes

Sweet williams – particularly the dwarf variety – have been used with great success in window boxes. The boxes must, however, be well drained and they should be filled with JIPC or Alex Soilless. Plant in September and the boxes will be beautiful the following June or July.

Varieties

This heading must be used as a kind of umbrella to include not only the varieties we know today but many of the hybrids which were introduced during the last century. A list will be found in Chapter 13.

Hybrids

SWEET WIVELSFIELD

Years ago Montague Allwood introduced a new race, which he called the Sweet Wivelsfield, produced as a result of crossing the sweet william with a hybrid race of pink known as dianthus x allwoodii. It has the good characteristics of both parents, i.e. a bushy habit of growth about 12–18 in. high, nice strong foliage, a wide range of attractive, coloured flowers and a really long flowering period, especially if the dead flowers are removed. Later the Henfield strain was produced as the result of careful selection; this is double flowered.

The seed of Sweet Wivelsfield is usually sown out of doors in April or May and the plants then flower in the late summer and autumn. Some gardeners sow the seed in August or early September with the idea of allowing the plants to over-winter and getting them in flower the following May and June. Sweet Wivelsfields can, of course, be grown in pots in a cool greenhouse.

RAINBOW LOVELINESS

This is included because it has Sweet Wivelsfield blood in it; it grows to a height of 15 in. and doesn't need staking. It is very popular because of its glorious scent. It produces very feathery, fine flowers which have a mist-like appearance. There are colour selections of this strain; white – a true white with a faint green eye; blue – a rich lavender blue; and crimson – a lovely shade. It is a wonderful plant for setting out at the base of a window, as its perfume wafts into the house. It is even more beautiful the second year. It flowers from June to October.

DELIGHT

This has Sweet Wivelsfield blood in it also. It doesn't grow more than 6–9 in. high, starting to flower in the early summer and continuing through the frosts of October. It is excellent for rock gardens, or where an edging plant is needed, because it is short and erect. It is indeed like a baby sweet william.

PINK BEDDER

This is another plant out of the Sweet Wivelsfield stable. It grows about 9 in. high and produces masses of salmon pink flowers from June to October.

RED BEDDER

This is considered the best red bedding-out variety known. The flowers are a glorious red, the trusses are large and it makes a wonderful show from early summer to late autumn. It can easily be raised from seed sowing.

DIANTHUS X MULTIFLORUS

The experts say that this was produced as the result of a deliberate cross between the sweet williams and *d. plumarius*. The variety Roseus is probably the best known today – it is a deep rose pink. It likes a sunny spot in the rock garden and it grows about 9 in. high. It is propagated by layers or cuttings and flowers throughout the summer.

DIANTHUS X BARBATUS MAGNIFICUS

This is the beautiful old true double crimson sweet william which must be grown in a well-manured bed and should be dug up and divided every 2 or 3 years. It grows 9 in. high, flowers from early July to the end of August and likes the soil where it grows to be top dressed with sedge peat about the middle of June. The flowers are, of course, deep crimson and really double.

Rust (*Puccinia lychnidearum*)

Diseases of the dianthus family in general are discussed in Chapter 11, but there is one particular disease – rust – which can be a serious problem with sweet williams, so I have included it here.

Brown tufts or pustules will be found on the leaves of the plants. In bad cases the foliage will turn brown and dark. Remove badly affected leaves the moment they are seen. Spray the plants with colloidal copper or diluted Bordeaux mixture in April, making certain that the under sides of the leaves are wetted as well as the upper sides.

11 Pests and diseases

Carnations, like most other plants, are subject to pests and diseases; half the battle of trying to cure is being able to diagnose the trouble correctly and to understand the underlying principle of the remedy. It is no use, for instance, trying to kill by using a poison spray a pest which obtains its food by pushing its proboscis into the middle of the leaf in order to suck the sap. Creatures that can be killed with poison deposits are those like caterpillars which actually eat the leaves and stems. Sucking insects, on the whole, have to be exterminated by a spray or fumigant like nicotine, which paralyses their nerve centres. It is always worthwhile using a magnifying glass so that a tiny insect or the spores of some disease can be seen more clearly.

Prevention

Prevention is always better than cure and everything should be done to grow the plants properly. Under glass, this means using the right compost, and in the open it means having plenty of organic matter in the soil. There should never be any dirty corners in the garden or in the greenhouse. It pays to face the greenhouse walls with concrete, so that there are no nooks or crannies in which pests can lurk. If there is a water storage tank in the greenhouse, it may need cleaning out thoroughly. Perhaps it needs whitewashing thickly on the inside or maybe scrubbing down with a 2 per cent solution of formaldehyde.

Diseased material should never be allowed to lie about the soil or in the greenhouse. It is always better to take up one whole plant and destroy it rather than to leave it in position with disease spores spreading. Weak plants are always much more likely to be attacked than those which are sturdy and strong.

Be sure to feed correctly so that the plants grow robust and strong. Use fertilizers with an organic base, which not only contain the three normal plant foods – nitrogen, phosphates and potash – in the right proportions, but also many of the trace elements which plants need. If carnations are given too much nitrogen they grow soft and will be more subject to pests and diseases. See that the feeds are always properly balanced.

Always give carnations plenty of room for proper development. When the plants are crowded together, they naturally suffer from diseases. Drainage is important. No members of the dianthus family can grow properly if their roots are standing in water. It is just as bad for the roots to be deep in water in winter as for them to be thoroughly dried out in the summer. Plants growing in pots should, therefore, be properly crocked, while those growing in soil should have plenty of drainage material buried well down if there is any sign of waterlogging.

Never attempt to propagate from poor stock. Never take cuttings from plants that have been weakened for years by being grown in soil entirely fed with chemical fertilizers. Be careful to propagate only from the best and healthiest plants each season. You can do much as a gardener to build up your own strong strain which suits the local conditions. Buy in your new stock as necessary from a really reliable nursery.

Don't be afraid to open the greenhouse ventilators when the weather is suitable. Generally, more trouble is caused by under-ventilation than by over-ventilation. Never allow the plants to exhaust themselves through an over-dry atmosphere; be prepared to water the paths and the staging of the greenhouse with the idea of keeping the atmosphere slightly humid. Syringing the under surfaces of the leaves will also help to reduce evaporation and keep down red spider.

Never forget that carnations dislike acid conditions; make sure that the correct alkaline-acid balance is maintained. This will usually mean adding some crude form of lime, such as ground chalk. Out of doors, adopt a rotational system so that the plants are not on the same piece of ground for more than 2 or 3 years. In the greenhouse, see that the soil is refreshed from time to time.

In fact, do everything possible to see that the carnations and pinks are growing happily on the right soil, with the right food, and with plenty of sunshine and air. Keep the ground cultivated shallowly so that there is no competition from weeds, and if necessary mulch the soil with sedge peat to the depth of ½ in. or so to provide fine organic matter and to preserve the moisture in the soil.

Fungus diseases

A number of diseases attack carnations. Fortunately, some of them are not very important, and the majority of those mentioned below cause trouble principally to carnations and pinks growing under glass.

RUST

Uromuces caryophyllinus. Unfortunately, this is a common trouble with carnations under glass. The infection usually starts on the lowest leaves but may spread rapidly over the plants under conditions which are ideal for the fungus. It is often bad when the plants are given too much water or when the temperature is kept too high. The disease is recognized by small brown spots with a blister-like appearance on the leaves. In bad attacks, these spots appear on the stems and flower buds as well.

Always avoid high temperatures and be very careful never to water excessively. Keep the temperature at about 55 degrees F, and avoid splashing as this will encourage the disease. Keep the atmosphere drier than normal and give plenty of air by opening the ventilators well.

Be sure to propagate only from healthy plants. Remove leaves which show serious infection. Aim to grow varieties which are less susceptible to this disease. Spray the plants with colloidal sulphur. Be sure to cut all the blooms which are out or opening out before applying either of these washes, to prevent the petals from becoming spotted.

RING SPOT

Heterosporium echinulatum. Pale circular spots are seen on the leaves, together with dark-coloured tufts or spores which are produced in abundance in concentric rings.

Hold the rose of the watering can as near the soil as possible, to avoid actually watering the leaves of the plants. Pick off seriously infected leaves the moment they are seen and burn them. Spray the plants over with colloidal sulphur, as advised for rust.

CARNATION MILDEW

Odium sp. A whitish powder is seen all over the surface of the infected leaves. This powder is found also on the calyxes and on the petals of the flowers themselves. It is caused by poor cultural conditions and often occurs when the soil has been under water.

Buy a fine sulphur dust and apply it all over the plants with a dust gun.

CARNATION STEM ROT

Fusarium culmorum. This soil fungus which is commonly found in

earth can cause serious losses (a) as propagation takes place,
and (b) when the young plants are first put out. The bottoms of
the stems go rotten and a blackish-brown stain can be traced
right up the stem. Sometimes, if wounds are made by insects or
by gardeners, other parts of the plants may be affected.

Some gardeners believe that the application of lime to the soil
helps, if used at 7 oz to the square yard. Others are of the
opinion that an over-rich soil will encourage the trouble, as will
deep planting. (See also wilt, below.)

VIRUSES

There are two viruses which can attack carnations – mosaic and
streak. Mosaic is usually seen as pale green mottling, and streak
as yellowish, white or reddish spots and streaks on the leaves,
which may cause them and the flower stems to die. The trouble
is invariably seen first in the spring and is especially noticeable
on rooted cuttings. Both these viruses are aggravated as the
plants get older, by poor soil conditions.

Because streak is transmitted by aphids, keep these at bay by
spraying. Mosaic is transmitted on the knives and fingers of
whoever does the stopping and picking. Dip knife blades in a 2
per cent solution of formaldehyde, and if you are a smoker wash
your hands in carbolic soap before working with carnations
(there is a danger of the virus in tobacco stain causing infection).

Be sure to propagate only from absolutely healthy plants.
Any carnations thought to be infected by either of these viruses
should be burned. Look for the signs in the spring because in
autumn and winter the symptoms are invariably mild.

WILT

Verticillium cinerescens. Unfortunately, this is usually coupled
with stem rot. The carnations will be seen to go yellow and wilt;
sometimes this trouble starts with one stem only, while on other
occasions it seems to be the whole plant that suffers at one time.
The disease enters through the base of the stem or the roots and,
in cases where infection is really severe, dieback may result in
the upper shoots when cut.

The trouble is always in the soil and this must either be
sterilized or, if it is in the greenhouse, carried outside and new
soil put in. The reason I have advised special compost for
carnations is largely because of this disease.

Over-watering may cause the trouble, which, of course can

easily be carried over from year to year in the cuttings of the plants. Once the disease has occurred, all cuttings taken should be dipped in a solution of colloidal sulphur before being struck. Thorough cleanliness, of course, is essential, and even though the top soil may be sterilized there is always a possibility that the subsoil is the source of the trouble. Infected plants should always be carefully dug up and burned.

SMUT

Ustilago antherarum. A soot-like substance appears in the centre of the flowers which then open up as if to show off the trouble. This disease is right inside the plant and cannot be cured. Attacked plants can usually be recognized because they are more bushy and because the buds have a more squat appearance. The stems, too, are usually thinner.

Pull up infected plants and burn them. Be careful to eradicate all weeds for the disease may live on these, and once again be sure only to take cuttings from healthy plants. Other plants like silene and lychnis may be attacked by this disease. Eliminate these if necessary and control weeds thoroughly.

BRANCH ROT

Pseudo-discosia-dianthi. This is sometimes called leaf rot because the disease attacks the bases of the leaves which show greyish spots. Later these spots seem to turn rotten and appear brown and moist.

This is a fungus disease which loves low temperature conditions and high humidity. It helps if the temperature can be raised, say to 55 or 60 degrees F. The plants must be watered with care; direct the spout of the watering can into the pot and don't let any splash on to the path or staging. Cut out the infected shoots with a sharp knife and spray the plants with a colloidal copper wash.

LEAF SPOT

Septoria dianthi. The disease usually starts on the lower leaves and then spreads upwards. Light brown spots appear with browny purple edges to them. In bad attacks the tips of the leaves start to die.

Everything should be done to keep the leaves dry. Avoid syringing over the plants, give plenty of ventilation and keep the temperature at about 55 degrees F to ensure a buoyant atmosphere. The trouble may be expected in a sunless, wet summer.

Apply a fine sulphur dust with a dust gun over the leaves of the plants. It is better to do this than to use a wet spray.

DAMPING OFF

Fusarium species. The stems of the cuttings collapse, with the result that roots do not grow. It is a disease which attacks young seedlings and cuttings and, once it has attacked the baby plants at soil level, they promptly collapse. It is most important, therefore, to use clean sharp silver sand for every batch of cuttings taken. If a substance like vermiculite is chosen as the rooting medium it must be thoroughly washed in boiling water before being used again.

In the case of seedlings, be sure to use JIPC or Alex Soilless compost which, of course, entails sterilizing the soil. Be very careful about the water. This must be clean or the sterilized soil may become reinfected. If you think the water may be contaminated, boil it before using. Sow in a sterile compost.

Don't syringe the cuttings over in dull weather if the disease is seen, but keep the atmosphere on the dry side. Good sunlight and fresh air are an excellent antidote to damping off.

Insect pests

PREVENTION

In combating both fungus diseases and insect pests, it does of course help greatly if the greenhouse can be kept perfectly clean. All the woodwork, for instance, should be painted white, preferably in a hard gloss paint which encourages maximum reflected light. Direct sunlight is first class and reflected light is very valuable. See that you have them both. Before painting the staging and sash bars, burn one or more sulphur candles in the house, to kill all the disease spores that may be lurking in the cracks.

Some people prefer to wash down the inside of the house thoroughly with a 2 per cent solution of formaldehyde. Care must be taken, however, not to inhale the fumes. Once the inside has been thoroughly cleaned out and painted (remember that if there is an inside tank for water storage this must be cleaned and painted also) the outside of the house can be tackled. All the glass will need washing thoroughly with hot water and detergent. The outside woodwork will also need to be painted, for unfortunately some pests like red spider hibernate on the ridging caps of the greenhouse and then wander down later on in the summer to attack the plants.

There are probably even more pests than diseases of carnations, especially under glass. Fortunately, insecticides will give
adequate control and strong, hardy plants, well grown, have
some natural resistance to insect pest attacks. Out of doors, of
course, carnations may be attacked by numerous pests which go
for all kinds of plants. Members of the dianthus family, for
instance, are not immune to slugs, woodlice, wireworms and the
like.

CARNATION FLY

Delia brunnescens. This pest is sometimes called carnation maggot or carnation leaf miner. It attacks plants, cuttings and layers
both in the open and under glass. It has also been seen on sweet
williams. Flies somewhat smaller than the normal house fly lay
their eggs on the upper surface of the leaves. These hatch out in
10 days and the tiny maggots which appear burrow into the
foliage. There they produce the typical blisters. When fully
grown the maggots leave the plants and pupate in the earth.
They are usually two generations a year.

Use a nicotine spray in late April or early May with the idea
of killing the baby maggots and discouraging the female flies.
Affected leaves may be picked off and burned. If the weed
known as ragged robin grows in your garden, eliminate it
because it is an alternative host.

CARNATION TORTRIX

Cacoecia pronubana. The caterpillars of this moth feed on the
leaves and flowers, often boring into the flower buds. They often
twist and roll the leaves together with fine silky threads. The
caterpillars are usually olive green, while the adult moths which
fly at night have grey fore-wings and orange hind-wings. After
feeding for 3 months, the caterpillars will pupate inside a dense
web on the plant where they turn black. A fortnight later the
adult moths emerge and start the second brood. There are
certainly two generations a year, but, as these may easily over-
lap, attacks may continue over a long period.

Spray the plants with a pyrethrum wash the moment you see
the trouble, or, if preferred, use a fine derris dust in a dust gun.
Repeat the doses at three-weekly intervals during the summer
as a precaution.

You can do a lot of good in the very early spring by actually
picking off the baby caterpillars, and squashing between thumb
and forefinger the flattish egg clusters which may consist of 200

eggs. Look for these on the leaves or stems and even on canes if they are used.

APHIDS

Myzus persicae. Aphids are found on leaves, flower buds and stems, sucking the sap. They can ruin carnations and pinks out of doors as well as under glass. Some of the aphids appear to transmit virus diseases as they spread from plant to plant. They usually appear in the spring and if they are not controlled they will persist throughout the season.

In the open, spray with a pyrethrum insecticide or use a good nicotine insecticide on a warm day. Liquid derris has also proved useful, if used in the early stages.

Under glass, it is a simple matter to use a smoke pellet which can be lit in the late evening after the greenhouse has been closed down. Follow this fumigation with another 5 days later to catch any adults which may have hatched out after the first treatment.

RED SPIDER

Titranychus telarius. This is probably the most serious pest of carnations and particularly so under glass. It attacks leaves, which turn a rusty dull colour, and in serious cases the plant will die. On carnations all stages of the mites are distinctly reddish, a fact which distinguishes them from other red spiders which attack many differing plants in the greenhouse. When red spider mites attack carnation flowers, the blooms become quite disfigured and ugly.

The mites usually hibernate in the walls and woodwork of the greenhouse as well as in canes and pieces of straw. They can live throughout the winter without feeding; breeding, however, is continuous throughout the spring and summer and it is only in late October or early November that hibernating females are produced.

Fumigate the greenhouse with a red spider smoke which can be bought in pellet form ready to light. Follow the first fumigation by a second one in 8–10 days' time, or spray liberally with a derris wash. Some people use Malathion aerosols with success.

The best method of control is by a fast moving, orange parasite, *Phytoseiulus persimilis*, that eats red spider. Each female parasite lays approximately 50–60 eggs, at 3–4 per day. They hatch in 2–3 days and there are three immature stages. The complete life-cycle takes 7 days, about half as long as that of the red spider mite. This parasite does not feed on plant material and its survival is entirely dependent on the maintenance of the red spider mite population. It is very efficient at searching for its prey and each female will devour up to 5 adults or 30 eggs and young per day. Unlike its hosts, the predator does not normally hibernate in the winter, and must be reintroduced each year as required. There should be 100 predators per house, unless the infestation is *very* high, when 200 should be introduced. The address of the suppliers of these predators is given in the Appendix.

THRIPS

Thrips tabaci. Thrips are tiny long insects, and the best way of discovering whether carnations are being attacked by them is to hold a clean white handkerchief or rag near a plant, tap the stem and then see whether any little black dots appear on the material. If examined under a magnifying glass they will be seen to be brownish black. The creatures can breed all the year round in the greenhouse – the eggs hatch out in 8 days and the whole life-cycle only takes about 24–30 days.

They can hide in the opening flowers or in crevices in the soil; they are especially undesirable on darker-coloured flowers because bleached spots occur on the petals. Thrips are sucking insects and their eggs are laid in the calyx of the flower, as a rule, while it is still in bud, the dark and pink varieties being the worst affected. The insects flourish in high temperatures and thus do the bulk of their damage in the summer and autumn.

Never allow the temperature of the greenhouse to run too high. Never let the soil, or the atmosphere, be too dry. Cut and burn flowers seen to be badly infected.

Apply a good pyrethrum spray to the upper parts of the plants once a fortnight, or fumigate the greenhouse. Some gardeners have had success by using powdered naphthalene at the rate of 5 oz to 1000 cubic feet. This is applied along the paths early in the evening before the greenhouse is closed down. Half an ounce of nicotine per 1000 cubic feet can be used with great effect in conjunction with the naphthalene.

OTHER PESTS

There are a number of other pests which will attack carnations, like slugs, woodlice, millipedes, cut worms, earwigs and wireworms. These are general pests because they attack a very large number of plants.

Wireworms may be kept at bay by working a pyrethrum dust into the soil at the rate of 1 oz to the square yard, 3 weeks before planting. Cut worms can be discouraged by using derris dust in June and again in September, at 2 oz to the square yard, and raking it in. Some people get rid of woodlice by keeping a toad in the greenhouse; if one of these is not available, using derris dust is recommended. Slugs can be killed with blue Draza pellets from the chemist.

A wireworm (greatly enlarged)

12 Carnations and pinks month by month

It is difficult to lay down hard and fast rules as to what must be done in a garden at any particular period, bearing in mind the climatic differences in various parts of Britain. Please, therefore, take the suggestions as a general guide to what should be done month by month. Some people like to have reminders to keep them up to date, and this chapter is specially for them.

January
Outdoor carnations should be resting and indoor ones should be cropping well.

OUT OF DOORS
If necessary do a little hand weeding among border carnations and pinks. If young plants were put in during the autumn, you may need to tread around them when the thaw comes after a severe frost, because in these conditions the plants tend to rise out of the soil.

UNDER GLASS
The perpetual-flowering carnations should be cut regularly if they are needed for indoor decoration. Pots that are being used for conservatory decoration should have their flowers cut back directly they die off.

Take cuttings of perpetual-flowering carnations, trying to get them all done by the end of the month. Later in the month potting compost should be prepared (or bought) and put under cover, so that it will be ready and warm when the struck cuttings are ready for potting.

Prepare or buy compost for seed sowing and put it in aluminium trays or seed boxes. Sow seeds, if desired, of blue dianthus, perpetual-flowering carnations and dianthus all-woodii.

Late in January the seed of giant Chabaud carnations may be sown.

February
The hours of daylight lengthen appreciably this month, so

86

Harvesting perpetual-flowering carnations

plants under glass tend to grow more, especially after the middle of the month.

OUT OF DOORS
A certain amount of hoeing and weeding among any members of the dianthus family growing in the open will be advisable, but only, of course, if the weather permits. It is often possible towards the end of the month to plant out some of the pinks and the most hardy of the carnations, but only if the soil is light and well drained and if the weather is kindly. (This is an instruction more for gardeners in the south than for those in colder parts in the north.)

Even in the rock garden, it is sometimes possible by the end of February to put out dianthus allwoodii alpinus as well as specimens of the various kinds of rock pinks.

UNDER GLASS

Sow some more giant Chabaud carnation seed in JIPC or Alex No-Soil compost.

Sow seed of the Sweet Wivelsfield and dianthus delight in John Innes or Alex No-Soil compost in aluminium trays or seed boxes; the idea is to have the plants well in flower early in the summer. Seeds of border and perpetual-flowering carnations can be sown this month also, if required.

The cuttings of perpetual-flowering carnations taken in January should now need potting on into their 2- or 3-in. pots. If you did some propagation in the autumn you may find that the plants are large enough to pot on into 6-in. pots.

As the weather gets warmer and daylight extends, plants need more water and this must be attended to persistently and carefully.

Watch out for both insect pests and diseases. Take precautions as described in Chapter 11.

March

The carnations should be flowering bravely in the greenhouse. It should be possible to give more ventilation now; care must still be taken about regular watering.

OUT OF DOORS

About the middle of the month, even in the heavier soils, it should be possible to plant nice young border carnations and other types of outdoor dianthus. In the rock garden it will help if limestone chippings are put around the plants to a depth of ¼ in.

In the case of carnations and allwoodii growing in borders throughout the winter, a certain amount of cutting back may be done if necessary and some fish manure given at 3–4 oz to the square yard. This can be lightly hoed in.

It is a great month for planting all kinds of pinks and remember that these make very good border flowers. The baby types of dianthus may also be planted in between crazy paving as well as between the stones of dry walls.

UNDER GLASS

Be very careful with watering this month – there may be a good deal of frost about. The sun may not be out and under such conditions carnations need a minimum of water. On the other hand, if it is bright and sunny, as it may well be for some days, water will have to be given.

Don't propagate any more perpetual-flowering carnations from cuttings after about the first week of March. It is better always to do this work in January and February. The one-year-old plants should now go into their 9-in. flowering pots in JIPC 2 or Alex Soilless compost.

Feed flowering carnations with fish manure, giving a tea-spoonful per pot or 4–5 oz to the square yard when the plants are growing in beds.

Pot on any perpetual-flowering carnations that seem to need it. If you started your plants off in 2-in. pots you will have to pot them on into 3-in. pots before the end of the month.

This is the month for stopping perpetual-flowering carnations. Take out the growing points right the way down to the fifth pair of leaves. Watch out for insect pests and diseases. Use JIPC or Alex Soilless compost to sow, if you wish, seeds of pinks and border carnations and almost any other type of dianthus you need.

April

April is an active month from the plants' point of view. The soil starts to get warm outside and plants in the greenhouse grow quickly. In the greenhouse the carnations should still be flowering well.

OUT OF DOORS

Hoe very shallowly around the pinks and border carnations and any other types of dianthus you are growing. In the rock garden there should be very little to be done other than hand weeding.

A number of plantings can be done – I usually plant giant Chabauds out during the second week of the month, in a nice sunny position. The plants then flower continuously from July onwards. Plant out also the Enfant de Nice, the Fleur de Camelia and the Benigna. Dianthus allwoodii may also be planted out in the open.

You can raise border carnation plants by sowing seed in a finely prepared bed in the open. Chabaud carnations can be raised in the same way and they flower very late as a result.

Some of the plants may need supports this month, especially if you are going to grow border carnations for exhibitions.

Aphids are usually troublesome from the second week of the month onwards, so be prepared to spray with nicotine.

UNDER GLASS

From now on the plants will undoubtedly need more water. Never let the air of the house get too dry so, if the weather is sunny and windy, be prepared to water the paths of the greenhouse through the fine rose of a can.

Stake or support plants as necessary. Carry out disbudding week by week as required. If any perpetual-flowering carnations were rooted in February, they will probably need stopping down to the sixth pair of leaves about the third week of the month.

In the south and south-west, if it is very sunny towards the end of the month, it may be necessary to spray the outside of the glass with Summer Cloud or a similar product, to give a very light shading.

May

If shallow, regular hoeings are carried out all through the month and right to the end of June, there will seldom be any weeds afterwards. You will still be picking carnations in the greenhouse, even if you have to wait until June for the border carnations.

OUT OF DOORS

Stake border carnations, and plant out another batch of them – the ones that were raised from seed sowing.

Sow sweet william seed in a fine seed bed this month, with the rows 6 in. apart.

Hoe among all dianthus plants. Some gardeners like to cover the soil this month with sedge peat to the depth of ½ in., which acts as a mulch and smothers weeds.

Give the pinks a feed of fish manure, applying this along the rows at 3 oz to the yard run, and lightly hoe it in.

It is quite a good idea to plant out some of the flowering specimens of perpetual-flowering carnations into a sunny bed in the open about the third week of the month.

UNDER GLASS

Sow border carnation seed in JIPC or Alex compost, in aluminium trays or seed boxes. Sow also Tige de Fer, Flamand and Fantaisie.

By the middle of the month it should be possible to let the boiler out or to turn off the electric heater and to grow the plants naturally. Those in the really cold parts of the north may have to go on using some artificial heat until the third or fourth week of the month.

Continue damping down greenhouse paths with the idea of keeping the atmosphere slightly humid, and remember that syringing over the leaves of the plants (always in an upward direction) does help to keep away red spider.

The perpetual-flowering carnations which go on in the autumn and winter in their pots are required to flower at that period should now be potted up into JIPC 2 or Alex compost,

'Amateurs Beauty', a perpetual-flowering carnation

using 8-in. pots. The plants that are well rooted in their 3-in. pots can go straight into the flowering pots without any intermediate potting.

Attend to any necessary staking and supporting. Remember the values of using stakes with movable rings.

If the greenhouse is crowded, it should be possible at the end of the second week to stand some of the younger perpetual-flowering carnation plants in the open in a sheltered place. They can remain here until they go back into the house for winter flowering. The only exceptions are the apricot and yellow varieties which are not quite as hardy as the other shades.

June

This is perhaps one of the nicest months of the year from the point of view of carnations. Though the spring flowering of the other plants will be over, many of the dianthus will be coming out fast. The gardener cannot relax – he must be very busy removing flower heads as they fade, hoeing among the plants lightly and carrying out routine sprayings, if necessary, to keep down pests and diseases. This can be a very droughty month so be prepared to water, using a sprinkler or rainer.

Many of the dianthus will be blooming in the rock garden or in the dry wall. It is a good plan to visit alpine nurseries to note types and varieties that you would like to add to your garden.

OUT OF DOORS

During the first fortnight pipings of the various pinks should be taken, to continue the supply of plants in the future. Cut off faded flowers fairly low down to encourage more bloom.

Continue supporting plants. Disbud regularly for really good blooms.

Watch out for the carnation maggot and spray as advised in Chapter 11. Take cuttings of most of the dianthus plants and strike them in sandy soil in a cold frame. This can continue, if necessary, until late in September.

If you want dianthus allwoodii to flower in the greenhouse during the winter months, flowering out of doors must be stopped at all costs.

Cut flowers of the Sweet Wivelsfield, any hardy carnations and all dianthus which have sufficiently long stems. This not only encourages further flowering but gives the plants the right kind of pruning.

Don't forget to feed the plants with an organic fertilizer like fish manure. This needs to be applied about the middle of the month at 3 oz to the square yard, and then lightly hoed in.

UNDER GLASS

Sow more seeds of border carnations as well as Tige de Fer, Flamand and Fantaisie. It is also possible to sow giant Chabaud carnations and Enfant de Nice if the idea is to over-winter the plants in a sheltered nursery bed or cold frame for flowering the following season.

Those who have cold greenhouses may have to give them a light shading with Summer Cloud or whitening, because the main bulk of the perpetual-flowering carnations will start to bloom this month. Such shading isn't usually necessary in the north.

Keep watering the perpetual-flowering carnations regularly and be guided by the weather rather than the date. Syringe over on hot days, but in dull weather tend to keep the leaves on the dry side. Everything possible must be done to see that the plants are kept growing erect. Feed with fish fertilizer once a fortnight, at a saltspoonful per 8- or 9-in. pot, or at 2 oz to the square yard if the plants are in bed.

July

Carnations will be in bloom out of doors and most of the dianthus will be making a good show in the rock garden.

OUT OF DOORS

Continue to take pink pipings; some of them may be struck in sandy soil in a shady spot in the open but many, especially the hybrids, are better struck in sand in a cold frame. About the third week of the month, border carnations may be layered as they become ready and this work can easily continue for a fortnight or more.

You can sow seed of Chabauds out of doors this month, for over-wintering under cloches.

Continue to disbud border and perpetual-flowering carnations.

The cottage carnations which were planted last autumn will go on flowering until the late autumn and needn't be layered unless absolutely necessary.

If you have raised seedlings under glass you can now plant them out with safety.

Support plants as necessary, and keep hoeing shallowly to

keep down weeds. It is always better to mulch and hoe than to water and, in fact, watering must always be the last resort.

All types of dianthus should be flowering well in July, and as the blooms fade the stems should be cut down almost to their base.

You can start to layer border carnations; then they get well established before the winter.

UNDER GLASS

Continue to sow the seed of border carnations in JIPC or Alex compost. Naturally these plants will flower later than those raised from seed sown in May, but succession will be assured.

Attend to perpetual-flowering carnations regularly (disbudding, feeding, watering, etc., as advised for June). The same rules apply to syringing; do this in very sunny weather to reduce transpiration and prevent red spider. Syringing isn't necessary during a dull, cold period.

It may be necessary to shade the outside of the house with Summer Cloud or whitening if the sun is very hot.

August

Much of the layering of border carnations and dianthus should be carried out in the first two weeks – it is a mistake to wait until September. There will be plenty of carnations in bloom in the garden, and *dianthus deltoides* will be at its best in the rock garden.

OUT OF DOORS

Carry out layering of border carnations and cottage carnations. If the month is very dry, you will need to water the soil in which the roots of the layers are forming.

Continue hoeing lightly among the plants to keep down weeds, unless you applied a sedge peat mulch earlier.

Keep cutting back the flowers that have bloomed; this prunes the plants and keeps them dwarf and compact. Never allow any dianthus to seed because this exhausts them and stops them flowering.

Some people think that they ought to water their outdoor carnations continually in August and this is a great mistake. Everything should be done to prevent the soil becoming compacted. If is far better to mulch and to reduce watering to an absolute minimum. If water has to be given, use a sprinkler rather than a bucket – as the drops of water are thrown into the air they become aerated.

UNDER GLASS

It may be necessary to pot on some of the perpetual-flowering carnations into larger pots if they appear to be pot-bound.

A little Summer Cloud or whitening sprayed on to the sunny side of the house may do good, especially where pastel-coloured carnations are being grown.

This is a very bad month for red spider and everything possible should be done to keep down this pest. Syringing over the leaves helps; so does using a naphthalene gas.

Continue to water the paths through the fine rose of a watering can, to keep them dampened down, if the weather is very dry and hot. Water the plants themselves as necessary but be most careful not to over-water.

September

In the greenhouse, perpetual-flowering carnations should be at their best again and, out of doors, cottage carnations should still be producing masses of flowers.

OUT OF DOORS

Do not do any more layering now, examine the layers that were made early in August, and if rooting has taken place fully the young plants may be severed from their parents. The alternative is to plant the struck layers into their flowering quarters in the open. Border carnations can be potted up into 3-in. pots this month and live happily in a cold frame or under a cloche until planting out time comes, either in October or the following spring. It is better in wetter districts to over-winter in cloches or frames.

About the third week of the month, pinks and dianthus allwoodii can be planted out in the open. I have planted border and cottage carnations during the fourth week of the month with great success, even as far north as Cheshire.

The cuttings of dianthus taken in frames should by now have struck, and the plants can be set out in their permanent quarters or, if necessary, can be potted up for over-wintering under dutch lights or cloches.

UNDER GLASS

The seed of Sweet Wivelsfield and dianthus delight can be sown in JIPC or Alex No-Soil compost in special aluminium trays or seed boxes, with the idea of potting up the specimens afterwards for spring flowering in the greenhouse.

If you are growing the Chabaud carnations Enfant de Nice and Fleur de Camelia, you may like to pot up some of the best of the plants at the end of the month in JIPC 1 or Alex compost, and put them for the time being in a cold frame. About the middle of October they can go in the greenhouse and may flower during the winter.

Do not stop any of the perpetual-flowering carnations now, but cut back some of the healthiest plants fairly hard with the idea of producing good cuttings to raise healthy stock.

Watch out for pests and diseases, in particular red spider.

Any damping down that has to be done because of hot weather should be carried out in the morning and at midday. Do not damp down in the afternoon or the house may be in too moist a condition for closing down in the evening.

Towards the end of the month, pot carnations growing in the open should be taken into the greenhouse, and by the third week it is necessary to start heating the greenhouse again, especially in the north.

The cuttings of various types of dianthus that have been taken earlier can now be potted up into 3-in. pots if necessary.

October

From the gardener's point of view winter starts this month. Fortunately, carnations are very hardy and there is no need to be unduly worried. Cottage carnations may easily go on flowering until well into October, while perpetual-flowering carnations will be producing plenty of flowers under glass.

OUT OF DOORS

During the first fortnight, most of the hardy border carnations and cottage carnations can be planted out in a sunny position in well-drained soil.

The layers that have rooted can either be potted up or go into cold frames or can be planted out in the open. Dianthus all-woodii can be planted in the open.

Carry out what may be the last light hoeing and weeding of beds out of doors. Cut back any straggling border carnation plants and those of any other type of dianthus, to keep them compact.

UNDER GLASS

Perpetual-flowering carnation—'Serenade'

Many of the annual carnations can be sown in October with the idea of growing the plants on slowly in the greenhouse and then

Hanging or pendulous carnations outside a house in Zürich

Hardy border carnation—'Downs Royal'

'Chintz', a perpetual-flowering carnation

planting them out in the open the following April. I have treated Sweet Wivelsfield and *dianthus heddewigii* like this with great success.

The greenhouse must be heated to a constant temperature of about 45 degrees F, or the carnations won't prosper. They need a buoyant atmosphere and plenty of fresh air; it is seldom necessary – except in thick fog or during a very hard frost – to close the ventilators completely at any time.

Continue to keep your eye open for pests and diseases.

If you live in the north or in Scotland you can start to take cuttings of perpetual-flowering carnations towards the end of the month. Gardeners in the south, however, should always wait until December or early January.

Feed the plants: those growing in the border should have fish manure at 3 oz to the square yard, and each 8-in. pot can be given a small teaspoonful. It will probably be necessary to water the food in.

November

See that the outdoor plants are all right before they have to face the winter on their own. After this month, most of the work is done under glass.

OUT OF DOORS

All the rooted layers of outdoor carnations should be potted up into 3-in. pots and safely in their cloches or under dutch lights in frames. There is still time, as a rule, to plant young border carnations out in the open during the first week of the month.

Make certain that outdoor dianthus and carnations have been cut back and that all the flower heads have been removed almost down to their base. Put some more limestone chippings around the dianthus in the rock garden. Remove supports from border carnations and cut back pinks if necessary. Try and do all this work as early in the month as possible.

UNDER GLASS

Sow seed of Chabaud carnations in JIPC or Alex Soilless compost. Pot up some of the border carnations into 6- or 8-in. pots and bring them into the greenhouse during the first week.

Sow the seed of Sweet Wivelsfield in JIPC if you want to grow some in pots under glass.

During the first week, be sure to wash off any Summer Cloud or lime sprayed on the outside of the glass. If there are bad foggy periods which leave a grimy deposit on the glass, spray it over to keep it quite clean.

Be very careful with water during this month. Keep the temperature at night at 45 degrees F, though it may rise a little during the day if there is any sun. The great thing is to have good air circulation.

If you are intending to grow carnations in beds in the greenhouse, start to prepare them this month.

December

Many gardeners, during the first week of this month, will be preparing borders and beds to take carnation plants in the spring. Well-rotted compost will be dug in and the land will be left rough for frosts and cold winds to act on.

If you live in the north you may have to dig up your border carnations and put them in cold frames. Alternatively cover the plants *in situ* with continuous cloches. There are few areas, however, in which cottage carnations will not prove themselves perfectly hardy during the severest of weather.

Incidentally, the foliage of many of the dianthus look beautiful this time of the year.

OUT OF DOORS

There is nothing to do out of doors this month except to look over the plants as necessary and tread down the soil around any newly-planted specimens that may have got loose as the result of a quick thaw after a severe frost.

UNDER GLASS

Pot on Sweet Wivelsfield and dianthus delight into the 3-in. pots in which they are to flower; if the house is crowded it is possible to leave this until January.

Any northern gardeners who have rooted perpetual-flowering carnations in October or November should now be able to pot them up into 2-in. pots.

Disturb very lightly the top ¼ in. of soil on the tops of pots in which carnations are growing, and about the middle of the month give a little feed as advised in October. Cultivate in a similar manner perpetual-flowering carnations growing in beds.

Keep the temperature of the house at 45 degrees F at night and try and keep the ventilators open all the time if possible, closing them at night only when the weather is freezing.

Take cuttings of perpetual-flowering carnations, if necessary, from healthy strong parent plants.

13 List of varieties

Border carnations

SELFS (SINGLE COLOUR)

Apricots

Bookham Apricot	Soft shaded self, strong grower.
Border Orange	Attractive orange self, large blooms with firm petals.
Clunie	Fine form, very popular.
Downs Apricot	Creamy, well-proportioned flower, robust.
Flambeau	Orange flame, easy to grow, bright variety.
Loyalty	A short compact habit of growth.
Lustre	Golden, a charming variety.

Crimson

Black Douglas Clove	Very dark crimson clove, strongly scented.
Bookham Grand	Rich crimson, robust grower, suitable for exhibition.
Border Crimson	Rich crimson, with a wiry stem, strong grower.
Crimson Model	Velvety crimson, flower weatherproof, good for exhibition.
Downs Clove	Medium-sized crimson, strong grower, marvellous perfume.
Fingo Clove	Dark crimson self, strong clove scent.
Gipsy Clove	Crimson self of strongest scent.
Matador	New crimson, rich colour and large flower of excellent formation, vigorous growth.
Oakfield Clove	Bold, glowing crimson, vigorous, clove scented.
Old Crimson Clove	Very popular, strong scented.
Orton Glory	Excellent crimson.
Oscar	New deep scarlet self.
Perfect Clove	Dark crimson, best of recent cloves.

| Shaston Supreme | Rich, deep crimson self of perfect form and good size, strongest growth, suitable for exhibition. |

Pink

Bookham Peach	A Malmaison pink shade, perfect habit.
Cherry Clove	Cherry rose self, strongest aroma.
Downs Cerise	Rich, glowing cerise pink, robust short grower.
Exquisite	Bright rose of good form and size, compact grower.
Frances Sellars	Glorious rose of good shape, strong stems, good habit.
Ibis	Bright carmine pink, delicate shades, strong grower.
Maybole	Neyron rose, exhibition flower of great charm.
Nautilus	True apple-blossom pink, very beautiful.
Pink Clove	Powder pink, exceedingly fragrant.
Pink pearl	Soft pink, with an apricot tone, very strong grower.
Salmon Clove	Deep rich salmon pink, old clove perfume, excellent.
Teviotdale	Ruby rose pink which holds its colour, an old variety.

Purple and mauve

Belle of Bookham	Colour officially known as *rose brûlé*, has a silvery sheen.
Downs Beauty	Deep mauve with an attractive sheen, good for exhibition.
Gala Clove	Deep purple, lovely clove perfume, compact and healthy.
Imperial Clove	Violet carmine, first-class clove.
Lavender Clove	Full-centred heliotrope with strong scent.
Leslie Rennison	Orchid purple with rose sheen or glow, clove scented.
Majestic Clove	Crimson purple with a strong perfume, nice grower.
Philip Archer	Light mauve.
Violet Clove	Violet carmine with a fine habit of growth.

Scarlet

Bookham Gleen	Fine rich scarlet, flowers perfectly formed, good exhibitor.
Downs Scarlet	Large vivid scarlet, compact grower, free flowerer.
Fiery Cross	Very brilliant scarlet, robust grower, good for exhibition.
Fusilier	Scarlet self, fine form and habit.
Pimpernel	Scarlet self, very free flowering.
Scarlet Fragrance	Bright scarlet, rich perfume, luxuriant blue-green foliage.

Hardy border carnations: (top) Eudoxia, (left) Lavender Clove, (right) Perfect Clove

Shaston Scarletta	Very bright scarlet self, finest form and size, robust growth.
Shaston Super Star	Vivid orange-scarlet self of perfect form and large size, robust habit of growth, good calyx, suitable for exhibition.
Tally Ho	Hunting scarlet, very popular.
W. B. Cranfield	Geranium scarlet, strong grower, good for exhibition.

Whites

Eden Side White	Clean white, good grower, good for exhibition.
Eudoxia	Pure white self, excellent habit.
Orton Purity	Excellent white
Spindrift	White self, robust habit.
Whitecliff	Pure white self, strong upright growth.

Yellows

Beauty of Cambridge	Sulphur yellow, largest size.
Brimstone	Bright yellow self.
Cowslip	Deep yellow, moderate grower, good foliage.
Daffodil	Daffodil yellow, lovely appearance, disbud lightly.
Sunray	Dresden yellow self, robust, best yellow.
Sussex Eclipse	Primrose yellow, striped mauve-purple, vigorous grower, stout stems about 29 in. long, no scent.

FANCIES

Autumn Tints	Buff, suffused russet orange, rich and distinctive.
Bookham Heroine	Shrimp pink and bright cherry red, good for exhibition.
Dawn Glory	Buff, overlaid lavender, good for exhibition.
Downs Flake	Turkey-red flaked, and striped maroon, lasts well when cut.
Downs Flame	Rich apricot marked with brilliant flame orange, nice short grower.

Downs Royal	Intense apricot-flecked soft rose, blooms 5 in.
Downs Sunset	Deep and light apricot-marked soft rose pink, strong grower.
Fancy Monarch	Smoke apricot with pale purple markings.
Harmony	Very deep lavender-grey barred with bright cerise pink.
Marmion	Orange-apricot suffused and striped brilliant scarlet.
Patricia	Beautiful new fancy, orange-apricot ground flaked pale lilac, habit of growth excellent.
Pat Phoenix	Pure white ground lightly marked pink, strong growth, perfect formation.
Portsdown Fancy	Exquisite flower, pale salmon minutely spotted scarlet, strong grower and good for exhibition.
Rameses	Lavender, apricot and scarlet, unusual and outstanding.
Raymond Court	Deep orange-apricot barred lavender-grey, good growth.
Shaston	Pure white, lightly ticked purple, large flowers of quite perfect form, strong growth.
Shaston Delight	Bright yellow edged and striped scarlet, good for exhibition.
Spangle	Orange-buff, suffused mauve, lovely fancy or large size.
Sussex Fancy	Rich crimson multiflecked with lilac purple, good strong stems.
Sweet Sue	Perfectly formed flower of pure white, overlaid rosy mauve, robust and vigorous in growth.

White ground fancies

Bookham Lad	Pure white ground, heavily striped scarlet, fine large flower of perfect form.
Bookham Lass	White, delicately barred tyrian rose.
Bookham Sprite	Snowy white base, heavily edged and

	striped glowing, deep cherry red, robust growth, perfect form.
Bookham Star	White-edged rose-purple, good grower.
Border Fancy	White lightly flaked red, strong erect grower.
Candy Clove	White striped rosy red, large, strongly scented flowers.
Dorothy Robinson	White delicately ticked with rosy scarlet.
Downs Souvenir	White marked with scarlet, beautiful blooms, robust.
Dunbar Clove	White evenly marked crimson, gloriously scented.
Egret	White delicately edged pale rose pink, attractive.
Lancing Lady	White heavily barred and edged brilliant scarlet, outstanding.
Lord Kitchener	White barred with blood red, old but dependable.
Mary Simister	Pure white ground marked with rose, bears perfect blooms on strong stems, outstanding.
Merlin Clove	White marked purple, gloriously scented.
Mrs Edmund Charrington	White heavily pencilled with lilac, beautiful.
Richard Hough	Pure white, marked lightly with rich purple, good for exhibition, strong growth.
Warrior	White marked blood red, perfect form, large and beautiful.

Yellow ground fancies

A. A. Sanders	Apricot, broadly edged and splashed heliotrope, lightly overlaid scarlet.
Bookham Prince	Pale amber yellow heavily marked and edged deep crimson.
Dainty	Primrose yellow marked soft pink, very attractive.
Downs Glory	Heavy rich crimson markings on a yellow ground, magnificent full bloom.

Downs Unique	Creamy yellow marked scarlet, full-sized flower.
Eden Side Fairy	Primrose yellow heavily edged blue-purple, most attractive.
Eden Side Glory	Rich buff-apricot ground, heavily suffused clear bright pink, stiff stems bear perfectly-formed flowers.
E. J. Baldry	Striking and beautiful, delicate canary yellow, ground edged and striped carmine violet, fine for exhibition.
Gavotte	Yellow edged and striped purple, finest form.
Heart's Ease	Yellow ground heavily flaked and edged rose.
John Ridd	Canary-yellow marked deep rose pink, robust grower.
Malvolio	Bright yellow ground with stripes of deep crimson, perfect form.
Mary McLeod	Buff-apricot heavily overlaid orange, excellent.
Mrs D. Gamlin	Evenly-marked and suffused bright clear cerise on rich apricot-yellow ground, perfect calyx.
Skirmisher	Yellow flushed mauve and flaked rose pink, short erect grower.
Surrey Fancy	Buff-apricot yellow, edged and striped rose pink.
Tony Cutler	Very attractive combination of colours, rich apricot-yellow ground suffused blood red.
Yorkshireman	Yellow-marked vivid scarlet, moderate compact grower.
Zebra	Maize-yellow striped deep crimson, fascinating.

PICOTEES

Crimson Frills	Yellow with a lovely crimson edge.
Dot Clark	Deep yellow, heavy rose pink edge.
Eva Humphries	White with a beetroot purple edge.
Fair Maiden	White with a light scarlet edge.
Fascination	White with a thin purple edge.
Fire Fly	Yellow heavily edged with crimson claret.

Margaret Lennox	Yellow heavily edged rose.
Patrick	White with a deep beetroot purple.
Santa Claus	Yellow with a purple edge.

FLAKES AND BIZARRES

Apricot Bizarre	Apricot splashed with carmine and rose.
Cherry Flake	Cherry cerise flaked with deep maroon.
Lilac Bizarre	Rosy lilac splashed with purple and mauve.
Pink Bizarre	Shell pink splashed with purple and rose, truly old fashioned.
Scarlet Flake	Orange scarlet flaked with deep chestnut.

Chabaud carnations

Aurore	Salmon pink.
Carmen	Raspberry red.
Etincelant	Bright red.
Fire Queen	A truly brilliant scarlet.
Giroflee	Scented mauve white.
Jeannes Dionis	Pure white.
La France	Soft pink.
Legion of Honour	Carmine terra cotta.
Magenta	Violet.
Marie Chabaud	Pure yellow.
Mikado	Slate violet.
Nero	Deep purple.
Orange	Orange sherbet.
Princess Alice	Salmon edged with white.
Reine Rose	Delicate rose.
Rose Queen	Bright rose.
Ruby Queen	Ruby red.
The Pearl	Flesh pink, mauve spotted.
White Queen	A truly snow white.
Yellow Queen	A sulphur yellow.

Heated greenhouse carnations

APRICOT AND YELLOW

Golden Rain	Clear canary yellow, free-flowering.

Harvest Moon	Buff yellow, popular, strohg stems.
Tangerine Sim	Orange self, lovely colour, large flower, good scent.
Yellow Dusty	Sulphur yellow, large flowers, vigorous grower.
Yellow Sim	Self yellow Sim, free-flowerer, disease resistant, good for winter flowering.

CRIMSON AND SCARLET

Allwood's Crimson	Large, crimson, heavy cropper, good grower.
Allwood's Scarlet	Scarlet, large flowers, keeps well, the only scented scarlet.
Crimson Velvet	Dark red, best for winter, perfect form.
Evelyn	Short growing, free-flowering, heavy cropper.
Joker	Free-flowering, excellent for buttonholes.
Jumbo Sim	Scarlet, heavy cropping, full flowers, good habit.
Red Sim	Scarlet in colour, produces many blooms all the year round.
Robert Allwood	Vivid scarlet, large flowers, full centre.
Sputnik	Crimson flowers, short habit of growth, good for pots.
William Sim	Improved, a good red, strong grower, no split calyxes.

PINK

Bailey's Splendour	Good compact pearl-pink blooms, strong but compact grower, flowers well in winter.
Crowley Sim	Pale pink, full compact flower, good grower.
Dusty Rose	Attractive full flower, rose pink, shortish habit and good stem, does not fade.
Edward Allwood	Beautiful pink, liable to fade in sunshine, large blooms, vigorous grower, clove perfume.

Keefer's Cherie	Salmon pink, sturdy grower, outstanding perfume, strong stems.
Lena	Salmon pink, nice shaped flowers.
Monty's Pale Rose	Attractive pale rose pink, nice perfume, strong calyx and stem, habit good, colour of foliage almost perfect.
Monty's Pink	Medium salmon pink, strong calyx, good perfume, disease resistant, free-flowering.
Pink Mist	Gorgeous lavender pink, with thin purple stripes, heavy producer.
Pink Sim	Beautiful pink sport of William Sim, strong grower.

PURPLE AND MAUVE

Doris Allwood	Salmon rose shaded with French grey, gloriously perfumed, good grower.
Persian Pink	Far more a mauve than a pink, strong grower, free-flowerer.
Purple Frosted	Light purple, strong perfume, strong stems, good for pots.

WHITE

Allwood's Cream	Lovely cream, scented type.
Fragrant Ann	Shapely pure white, nice habit, excellent perfume.
George Allwood	Pure glistening white, fringed flowers, gloriously scented, strong stems.
Icecap	Well-shaped large blooms, excellent winter producer.
Northland	Ivory-white, good habit for pot cultivation.
White Sim	White sport of William Sim, good grower, fast and prolific.

FANCIES

| Arthur Sim | Pale mauve with purple centre, excellent for pot cultivation. |

Cocomo Sim	Yellow, heavily striped with crimson, reliable variety, masses of bloom.
Dainty Maid	Pure white, wire-edged old rose markings, excellent pot plant.
G. J. Sim	Deep pink background with thin white stripes, produces many blooms.
Helena Allwood	White with deep strawberry markings, stiff stems, highly scented.
Pigalle	White, flaked and edged violet, strong stems, good calyxes.
Zuni	Cerise flecked with maroon-crimson, most unusual, good grower.

American spray carnations

Comtesse	Shocking red, robust and healthy.
Exquisite	Purple with a lighter edge to the petals.
Gris Royalette	Deep purple with a pale edge, pinkish.
Kristina	Butter yellow, an unusual colour.
Red Baron	Pure red, free flowering.
Sam Pride	Shocking cerise, very attractive.
Scarlet Miniqueen	Definite scarlet with a white edge.
Silvery Pink	Attractive light pink.
White Royalette	Pure white.

Malmaison carnations

Apricot Queen	An extremely large-flowered soft apricot, edged and flecked flame red.
Malmaison giant flowered	It is possible to get seed of a mixed re-selected strain of this type of Malmaison.
Old Blush	Glorious blush pink with a delicious scent.
Princess of Wales	Old salmon pink with a lovely perfume.
The Queen	Unusual terra-cotta colour with good perfume.
White Queen	A very sweetly perfumed white.

Outdoor pinks and allwoodiis

GARDEN PINKS

Andrew	Cerise sport of Timothy.
Daphne	Single, shrimp pink with deep eye.
Charles Musgrave	See Musgrave's Pink.
Dusky	Dusty pink with a clove perfume, double.
Earl of Essex	Rose-pink fringed, free-flowering, double.
Favourite	Pale rose pink with maroon eye, single.
Fimbriata	Creamy white, fringed, fragrant, double.
Fortuna	Rose-cerise self, free-flowering.
Freda	Blush mauve, free-flowering
Gloriosa	Large rose, highly scented, double (like a pink Mrs Sinkins).
Her Majesty	White, highly perfumed, fringed, double.
Inchmery	Shell pink, easy to grow, popular, double.
Ipswich White	Pure white, scented, strong grower, double.
Lilian	Heavy cropping white, good scent.
Little Old Lady	Crimson, edged white, sturdy, double.
Ludford Pink	Rose pink, free-flowering, dwarf, strong perfume, semi-double.
Messines Pink	Deep salmon pink, fully double, dwarf.
Mrs Sinkins	Pure white, free-flowering, cushion habit of growth, double.
Murray's Late Pink	White with a crimson eye and crimson lacing, semi-double.
Musgrave's Pink	White with a green eye, excellent for dry walls, single.
Old Fringed	White with extraordinarily strong perfume, semi-double, small.
Paddington	Shell pink with dark maroon eye, laced, dwarf, double.
Priory Pink	Blush mauve, perfumed, neat habit.
Red Emperor	Maroon with a crimson eye, bushy grower, good edger, double.

Robin	Bright scarlet, compact growth, short stem.
Rose Pink Mrs Sinkins	Rose pink with dark eye, more scent than Gloriosa, calyx splits badly.
Sam Barlow	White with purple eye, large flowers, double.
White Ladies	Satin-like white, delicious perfume, silvery-green foliage, compact grower, good edger, double.

LACED PINKS

A. J. Macself	See Dad's Favourite.
Constance	Pale pink-carmine lacing, vigorous and free-flowering.
Dad's Favourite	White laced with chocolate, dark eye.
Laced Joy	Rose pink, laced crimson, crimson eye, semi-double.
Laced Prudence	White ground, ruby lacing, dainty.
Laced Romeo	Creamy white with chestnut red lacing.
London Girl	White, laced black, black eye, very dwarf.
London Lovely	White with mauve lacing, dark eye.
Verity	Laced allwoodii, mauve-pink ground with velvet crimson eye.

Show pinks

Show Aristocrat	Pale flesh pink, buff eye, silvery foliage, good grower.
Show Beauty	Deep rose pink, maroon eye, symmetrical petals.
Show Bride	Salmon pink, azalea eye, good grower.
Show Celebrity	Deep rose pink with a maroon eye.
Show Charming	Pink with coral-red centre, semi-double.
Show Distinction	Cerise-crimson, with touch of fuchsia, no eye, excellent habit of growth, flowers well-shaped.
Show Emblem	Self pink, perfumed.

Show Enchantress	Salmon pink, no eye, perpetual flowerer, large, double.
Show Excellence	Clear pale fuchsia pink, with deep fuchsia eye, free-flowering, dwarf grower.
Show Glory	Orange-scarlet, free-flowerer, very striking.
Show Ideal	Cream with salmon red centre.
Show Magnificence	Apple blossom pink.
Show Paragon	Delicate pale pink, fine form.
Show Pearl	Pearly white, pale green centre, free-flowering, large.
Show Perfection	Rose pink, maroon eye, pretty foliage, scented.
Show Portrait	Pure crimson, free-flowering, perfect shape, double.
Show Satin	Shell pink self, delightful perfume, habit of growth compact.

Allwoodii

Alice	White, dark crimson eye, double.
Barbara	Crimson, no eye, free-flowerer.
Blanche	Pure white, compact grower, continuous flowerer, double.
Brian	Rose pink, speckled and flaked crimson-maroon, dwarf, double.
Bridesmaid	Shell pink with scarlet centre.
Bridget	Salmon pink, no eye, scented, semi-double.
Derek	Ruby crimson, free-flowerer, double.
Dianne	Salmon scarlet, very fine, sport of Doris.
Doris	Salmon pink, azalea pink eye, perpetual-flowering, glorious scent, semi-double.
Elizabeth	Deep salmon pink, scented, semi-double.
Fleur	Pale pink with deeper pink flakes.
Helen	Salmon pink, no eye, bushy grower, free-flowering, double.
Hope	White, crimson lacing, free-flowerer, scented, double.

Ian	Glowing crimson, compact grower, double.
Isabel	Cherry pink, chestnut eye, scented, semi-double.
Judy	Blush white, scarlet centre, short erect grower, free-flowerer, double.
Laura	Orange-scarlet sport of Doris.
Mandy	Cochineal pink, with paler edging.
Molly	Maroon-violet, edged white, pretty foliage, double.
Monty	Rose pink, chocolate centre, highly fragrant, semi-double.
Paul	Large full flowers of shell pink, veined with red.
Ruby	Deep wine or ruby shade, strong sturdy grower, excellent flower.
Rufus	Strawberry, deeper coloured eye, fringed, richly perfumed.
Susan	Pale pink, blackish purple centre, semi-double.
Thomas	Brick red with deep eye.
Timothy	Silver pink, flecked cerise, bushy plant, free flowering, perfect-shaped flower.
Vera	Light rose, reddish eye, waved petals, single.
Victor	Maroon-shaded pink, dwarf habit, double.

Imperial pinks

Cherry Ripe	Brilliant cherry pink self of fine form and size, an outstanding variety.
Crimson Ace	Very fine crimson self.
Flame	Vivid orange-scarlet.
Freckles	Dusky salmon, daintily flecked red, a flower of exquisite form and beauty.
Iceberg	Glorious white self of outstanding quality, fine for exhibition, grand bush habit of growth.
Lancing Lass	Beautiful rose pink with light red eye, free-flowering and perfect growth.

Peach	Lovely shrimp pink, with vivid scarlet eye.
Picture	Soft pink self.
Rosalie	Bright rose self.
Royalty	Between red and purple, a new colour, perfect habit.
Swan Lake	Fine white self, excellent habit of growth.
Treasure	Pale salmon self.
Winsome	Well named, rich deep pink with slight crimson eye. Perfect form grand habit of growth and pronounced perfume.

London pinks

London Glow	Ruby-red to black, edged pink, very beautiful, not perpetual-flowering.
London Poppet	White flushed with pink, ruby red lacing, ruby red eye, nice compact growth.

Dianthus allwoodii alpinus

Apollo	Rose-cerise flat double flower with a small maroon eye, 4 in.
Bombardier	Darkest crimson self, semi-double, smooth-edged petal, prolific alpine pink, 5 in.
Dainty Maid	Red with large crimson eye, petal white edging, fringed, 4 in.
Debutante	Only pink in this beautiful orange colour, fully double, at home among the alpine pinks, 7 in.
Dewdrop	White with a green eye, strongly perfumed, 6 in.
Diana	Bright magenta crimson, small darker eye, fringed, 4 in.
Echo	Maroon, single with a deeper eye, silvery foliage, 6 in.
Elizabeth	Rose with a distinct maroon eye, fringed and fully double, 4 in.
Fusilier	Bright crimson, dark centre, heavily fringed, compact in growth, 4 in.

Goblin	Blush salmon with a maroon velvety eye, 6 in.
Harlequin	Bright pink with large maroon eye, heavily fringed and compact in growth, 3 in.
Jupiter	Deep salmon pink double with a slightly deeper shaded eye, 6 in.
Mab	Reddish pink with a deeper eye, foliage silver, 6 in.
Mars	Bright crimson magenta with a smooth edged petal, semi-double, 6 in.
Nymph	Blush pink with a deeper pink eye, scented, 6 in.
Pinkie	Silvery rose, single, large flat flower, 4 in.
Puck	White with a maroon eye, 4 in.
Tinkerbell	Pale pink shading to tan in the centre, 6 in.
Wanda	White with a bold maroon eye, 4 in.

Dianthus deltoides

A. E. Bowles	Large ruby-coloured flowers, dark green leaves.
Albino	Pure white with lighter-coloured leaves.
Brilliant	Vivid cerise, pink, large flowers, compact grower.
Erectus	Rich red flowers on upright stems.
Icombe	Sugar pink flowers of enormous size, 9 in.
Little Jock	Short stemmed, double pink flowers with deeper eye, 4 in.
Mrs Clarke	Enlarged version of Mars, with brighter blooms, 9 in.

Alpine hybrids

These are found in catalogues under the heading 'dianthus hybridus x'.

| C. T. Musgrave | Neat, non-spreading plant, flowers pure white, large, scented, fringed and single, season July to August. |
| Dubarry | Matted, fine foliaged plant, rose flowered with centre crimson, |

	double, only 4-in. stems, season June.
Gingham Gown	Pretty hybrid with pink, maroon spotted blooms, 6–9 in. stems.
Gravetye Gem	Inch-wide flowers rose pink in colour, rounded, each petal with a maroon 'flash', 6 in.
Hidcote	Semi-double with deep red flowers on short stems over pads of grey foliage.
Inchmery	Double with soft pink flowers deliciously scented, 9–12 in.
Jordans	Compact, cushion-like plant, bears cerise-coloured flowers with an unusual greenish eye, stems 6 in. tall, season end May to end September.
La Bourbrille	(Sometimes called La Boulville in catalogues.) Nice neat alpine plant, can be used in the cracks of crazy paving, foliage very grey and plant extremely tidy, flowers pink, fringed and slightly scented, very easy to grow, season June to September.
London Brocade	Large patterned flowers, white and deep red, 12 in.
Miss Sinkins	The perfect baby of Mrs Sinkins which most people know. Pure white, double flowers, highly scented, very neat, stems 3 in. tall, season end May to September, excellent.
St George's	Rounded white flowers with pretty central area, large blooms, 6 in.
Spencer Bickham	Easy to grow, greyish-green dainty pointed leaves, flowers deep rose pink, scented, stems 3 in. tall, season end May to late July.
Waithman Beauty	Pink, flecked with a deeper colour, rounded flowers, 6 in.
White Bouquet	Cushions of dense grey and a profusion of neat white rounded flowers, 9 in.

Dianthus hybrids

Abbotsfordiana	Produces pale pink semi-double blooms on 8-in. stems from early July

	to mid-September, leaves truly silvery.
Adoree	Clear rose with large flowers, single, often 2 in. in diameter, stems 4–5 in. high, vigorous grower, flowers early and if the heads are cut down hard, gives a second blooming in the early autumn.
Alba Fimbriata	Pure white, sweetly scented, deeply-fringed hybrid, stems 9 in. tall, flowers June to end August, vigorous grower.
Audrey Pritchard	Rose pink flowers, clove scented, stems 8–9 in., flowers June to end August, tufted habit, double.
Blairside Crimson	Produces single flowers often over 2 in. in diameter on sturdy 6-in. stems, flowers deep pink with crimson eye, late May to end July, neat grower.
Cockensie	Comes from Scotland and said to be the true Montrose Pink, lovely double-flowered variety, pink, season July onwards, stems 1 ft high.
Delmondham Fairy	Looks more like a carnation than a pink, though it is definitely the latter, shrimp-pink flowers, scarlet eye.
Donizetti	Claret-coloured flowers with deep claret eyes, stems 9 in., flowers from June to August.
Duchess of Fife	Clear rich pink, strong grower, late summer flowerer, single.
Elsenham Seedling	Good vigorous grower, large, pink single flowers with darker eye, season late summer.
Floribundus	Rich rose pink, robust grower, stems 14 in., gorgeously scented, may flower too freely and so has to be restricted.
Fosteri	Rose crimson, leaves dark bronzy green, often over-flowers, generally subject to maggot attack, season July to August.

F. W. Millard	Dull crimson double flowers, stems 12 in., strong grower with ash grey leaves, seeds happily and the majority of the seedlings come true to type and colour.
Holmsted	Rose pink flowers 2 in. in diameter, stems 9 in. high, beautiful green foliage, usually increased by layering or cuttings.
Little Old Lady	Very old white variety, neat grower, extremely fragrant, vigorous, attractive.
Napoleon III	Cerise scarlet blooms, not a good grower, difficult to propagate because all the shoots seem to produce a bloom, season June, July, August.
Princess Christian	Pure white, chocolate centre zone, stems 1 ft, season June to August.
Raby Castle	Comes from Cumberland and is one of the oldest hybrids known, red, semi-double flowers, petals striped with black, gorgeously scented.
Windward Rose	Deep rose pink, ash-grey leaves, stem 6–7 in. tall, flowers throughout the summer, neat grower.

Sweet williams

Auricula-Eyed	Sometimes called the true old-fashioned sweet william, mixed seed contains carmine, crimson, scarlet, purple and white types on varying ground colours.
Auricula-Eyed Exhibition Strain	Specially fine strain of auricula-eyed sweet william, flowers richly zoned crimson on white ground.
Crimson Beauty	Bright crimson flowers with red-tinged foliage.
Dunnett's Dark Crimson	Produces dark crimson flowers with deep reddish-green foliage.
Giant White	Large flowered, snowy white variety with dark green leaves.
Indian Carpet	Dwarf sweet william, only grows 6 in.

	high, flowers are produced in a great variety of colours, practically all of them auricula-eyed.
Nigrescans	Deep crimson flowers and glorious dark purple foliage and stems, 18 in. high.
Pink Beauty	Extremely attractive rose pink, shaded salmon.
Scarlet Beauty	Very striking, brilliant orange or salmon-scarlet with dark green leaves.
Wee Willie	Ultra-dwarf and compact variety, excellent as edging plant, flowers have been known to appear 8 weeks after sowing, and may be crimson, rose pink, ruby or white, single blooms ¾ in. across but produced in clusters of four to six.

Glossary

Alpines Plants which come from mountainous or alpine regions; term used by gardeners to denote plants which are particularly suited to the rock garden.

Annuals Plants which live for 12 months only and therefore need to be raised from seed every year.

Axil The actual point of the angle between leaf and stem.

Ball The mass of soil, usually roughly in the shape of a ball, around the roots of young plants.

Biennial Plants which take 2 years to complete their life cycle – i.e. they do not flower until the second year.

Calcifuge Describes plants that prefer acid soils and are lime haters.

Calyx The green envelope which surrounds a flower before it opens; the flower sepals, in fact. (See *Sepal*.)

Compost Has two meanings: (1) a soil mixture for potting or for sowing seeds into, such as John Innes or Alex Soilless compost;
(2) vegetable refuse which is rotted down with an activator such as fish manure, poultry droppings or a special herbal preparation.

Crocks Pieces of broken pot placed over the drainage hole in a flower pot, to improve drainage.

Cultivar A variety which has been produced by man rather than nature.

Damping down Watering the paths of the greenhouse and sometimes the pipes in order to create moisture in the atmosphere.

Damping off Refers to a condition of seedlings when they fall over and decay, after being attacked by fungus diseases at soil level.

Disbudding The removal of superfluous flower buds so that the one left is improved in quality.

Hardening off The gradual exposure of plants to more airy, cool conditions. Plants from a greenhouse, for instance, may go into a frame before being planted out in the open.

Hardy Describes plants that are strong and sturdy and will grow quite uninjured throughout the winter without any protection at all.

Heel Small portion of older wood attached to the base of a cutting.

Humus Brownish colloidal jelly produced as the result of living matter being correctly rotted down through the work of organisms in the soil. Vegetable refuse forms compost (*q.v.*), and the compost when in the soil and acted on by living organisms produces humus.

Hybrid When a plant of one species is cross-fertilized with the plant of another species, a hybrid results.

Internode Section of the stem between two nodes.

Laterals Shoots which grow out of the sides of plants, as opposed to the leading shoots which are called leaders.

Mulching A covering of some kind of organic matter (in this book usually sedge peat) which conserves the moisture below, keeps the soil warm, prevents the effect of both drought and drying winds, and deters weeds.

Node A joint in the stem of a plant, which is usually somewhat swollen.

pH In Britain the extremes of soil acidity and alkalinity usually run between pH $8 \cdot 5$ and pH $4 \cdot 5$; pH 7 represents the neutral point; figures lower than 7 indicate the degree of acidity and figures above 7 show the degree of alkalinity. It will be seen that pH 4 is much more acid than pH 6. Test your own soil for acidity by using an indicating fluid which can be bought from chemists and garden shops, complete with instructions.

Perennial A plant which lives for many years.

Pinching or timing The removal of the growing shoots of a plant to a certain distance down.

Pistil The organ of the plant which bears the seeds. It includes the ovule with the style and stigma above.

Pricking out The transplanting of seedlings in their baby stage to other boxes or into special soil in frames.

Sepal Part of the calyx (*q.v.*), i.e. an individual leaf of the calyx.

Sport A growth which develops on its own on a plant, from which it is different in colour or form. Scientists call it a mutation.

Stamen The part of the plant which bears the male pollen.

Stigma The end of the pistil which accepts the male pollen, which is then passed down to the ovule.

Systemic An insecticide or fungicide which enters into the whole system of the plant.

Appendix

Classification of carnations

All carnations belong to the genus dianthus. The plants we grow today stem from three main parents: *dianthus caryophyllus*, *dianthus plumaris* and *dianthus barbatus*.

Under the heading of *dianthus caryophyllus* we have (1) border carnations, (2) cottage carnations, (3) perpetual-flowering carnations, (4) amateurs' carnations (a blend between perpetual-flowering and border carnations), (5) Malmaison carnations and (6) perpetual-flowering Malmaison carnations.

Under the heading *dianthus plumaris* we have (1) pinks, (2) laced pinks, (3) show pinks, (4) allwoodiis and (5) Herbert pinks.

Under the heading *dianthus barbatus* is the sweet william.

In addition there are hybrids which have resulted from crosses made with the dianthus and the allwoodii. They include (1) Sweet Wivelsfield, (2) Lancing pinks, (3) London pinks, (4) golden hybrids, (5) dianthus Delight and trailing dianthus Delight, (6) dianthus Loveliness and (7) imperial pinks.

In the annual dianthus group there are (1) Marguerite carnations, (2) Chabaud carnations, (3) Enfant de Nice, (4) camelia-flowered pinks and (5) Chinese or Indian pinks (*dianthus chinensis*) and particularly the heddewigii varieties.

The British Carnation Society

Readers who are interested in carnations and pinks should join the British Carnation Society. You will receive a copy of the Carnation Year Book and attend the shows of the Society.

Address letters to The Secretary, c/o The Royal Horticultural Society, Vincent Square, London SW1.

Suppliers' addresses

CARNATIONS

Allwood Bros (Hassocks) Ltd, Clayton Nurseries, Hassocks, Sussex.

Steven Bailey, Eden Nurseries, Sway, Hants.

Barkers, Whipley Nurseries, East Whipley Lane, Shamley Green, Surrey.

J. Hayward, The Chase Gardens, Purbrook, Portsmouth, Hants.

W. E. T. Ingwersen, Birch Farm Nursery, Gravetye, East Grinstead, Sussex (alpine hybrids).

Lindabruce Nurseries Ltd, 62 Kings Road, Lancing, Sussex.

George Roberts, Faversham, Kent (chabauds).

H. Smart, 52 Penderford Avenue, Claregate, Tettenhall, Wolverhampton.

Woodfield Bros, 7 Townsend Road, Tiddington, Stratford-on-Avon, Warwicks.

ALEX SOILLESS COMPOST

Michael Alexander, B.Sc., Alexander Peat Products, 1 Sea View Road, Burnham-on-Sea, Somerset.

RED SPIDER PREDATOR (PHYTOSEIULUS PERSIMILIS)

Organic Farmers and Growers Ltd, Longridge, Creeting Road, Stowmarket, Suffolk IP14 5BT

ORGANIC AND COMPOST GROWING: ADVICE AND SUPPLIES

The International Association of Organic Gardeners, Arkley Manor, Arkley, nr Barnet, Herts.

Index